HUGO DISTLER AND HIS CHURCH MUSIC

HUGO DISTLER

AND HIS CHURCH MUSIC

Larry Palmer

CONCORDIA PUBLISHING HOUSE

SAINT LOUIS · LONDON

Concordia Publishing House, St. Louis, Missouri

Concordia Publishing House Ltd., London, E. C. 1

© 1967 Concordia Publishing House

Library of Congress Catalog Card No. 67-20427

To my mother and father

• • •

who,
in a sense,
began all this

• • •

Acknowledgments

Grateful acknowledgment is hereby made by the author and the publisher to the following for permission to quote from their publications.

Associated Music Publishers, Inc., New York, for musical examples from Richard Wienhorst, *Missa Brevis* (p. 153).

Bärenreiter Verlag, Kassel and Basel, for quotations and musical examples from the published works of Hugo Distler (pp. 79—88, 90—101, 114—125, 127—131, 133—146); quotations from letters published in Bruno Grusnick, "Wie Hugo Distler Jakobiorganist wurde," *Musik und Kirche* (pp. 19—20, 22—25) and in Kurt Klein, "In Memoriam Hugo Distler," *Musica* (p. 31); and quotations from Erika Kienlin, "Erinnerungen an Hugo Distler," *Hausmusik* (pp. 57, 61).

Breitkopf & Härtel, Wiesbaden, for musical examples from the Distler motet *Herzlich lieb hab' ich dich, o Herr* (pp. 106—108).

Cantate Records Co., Greensburg, Pa., for the quotation from Oskar Söhngen, "Geistliche Chormusik von Hugo Distler," an introduction to Cantate Record No. T72714LP (pp. 104—105).

Hellmut Lehmann-Haupt for the quotation from his book *Art Under a Dictatorship*, published by Oxford University Press, New York (p. 72).

Higham Associates, Ltd., London, for the quotation from Osbert Sitwell, *Those Were the Days*, published by Macmillan & Co., Ltd. (pp. 13—14).

Vanguard Press, Inc., New York, for the quotation from *Collected Poems of Edith Sitwell* (p. 87).

The World Publishing Company, New York, for the quotation from Paul Collaer, *A History of Modern Music* (1961), translated by Sally Abeles from the second edition of the French text, *La Musique Moderne* (Brussels: Elsevier, 1955) (pp. 154—155).

PREFACE

Almost at the very beginning of the author's graduate study, in the fall of 1960, a chance mention of the music of a German composer named Hugo Distler excited a curiosity, which a cursory search through various dictionaries and reference books did little to alleviate. Grove's, for example, claimed Distler as "the most strongly individual personality among the younger German church composers," [1] but said little concerning the basis for this evaluation. Most books on 20th-century music did not even mention Distler's name, and the author became more and more curious about this young composer, whose music, it became increasingly apparent, was worthwhile and the basis for an entire cult in the composer's native Germany.

Thus began a study that has culminated in this biography of Hugo Distler, the first of this scope to be written in any language. A wealth of material concerning Distler is available in various German publications, but these articles are widely scattered and not available to most American readers. Fortunately the Sibley Musical Library of the Eastman School of Music possesses copies of the publication *Musik und Kirche* from the fourth year of publication (1932) through the early years of World War II, the period covering Distler's professional life. This periodical presented the author with his early material for this study. Many questions, however, could not be answered from periodicals only, and it became increasingly apparent that much more information would be required for a biography.

Thus, in the summer of 1962, the author visited Germany. In particular a visit to Lübeck was necessary; here Kirchenmusikdirektor Bruno Grusnick, an associate of Distler during the years 1931 to 1937, heads the *Distler-Archiv,* founded in 1952. He graciously placed at the author's disposal articles and theses gathered thus far by the *Archiv;* from him also came the document that has proved to be the most valuable for this study — the scrapbook of Distler's friend, the young pastor of the St. Jakobikirche in Lübeck, Axel Werner Kühl. In this personal collection of press clippings and programs Pastor Kühl preserved the bases for many of the personal observations concerning Distler; invaluable for this study was the nearly complete file of the St. Jakobi vesper programs from 1931 to 1937 contained in this book. That this volume should have survived is little short of miraculous; indeed, the fact that St. Jakobi, where Distler lived and worked during his Lübeck years, should be the only one of Lübeck's inner-city old churches to escape major disaster during the British air raid on the eve of Palm Sunday 1942 is also a bit of luck for which the author was humbly grateful.

The other invaluable source of information concerning Distler was his widow, Frau Waltraut Distler, who now lives in Marquartstein in Oberbayern. Her graciousness in inviting the author to her home, her complete willingness to share anything which could be of help (memories, scores, pictures), her hospitality, and her subsequent correspondence has placed the author so completely in her debt for this work that he can never hope to repay her generosity.

The author was thwarted in only one respect in the preparation of this biography. The letters of Hugo Distler, now being collected and stored in the *Distler-Archiv,* were not available for this study. An exact dating of many compositions as well as glimpses into the composer's private life remain, therefore, rare in this work.

To thank everyone concerned with this book would require another, the three major debts of gratitude are those to Frau Distler, KMD Grusnick, and Dr. M. Alfred Bichsel, who has borne the burden of consultation and reading and was responsible for the author's first acquaintance with Distler's works.

Special gratitude is also due Concordia Publishing House for an abiding interest in Hugo Distler and his works. Not only this book, the first biography of the composer, but a steadily increasing number of practical performing editions of Distler's works with English texts is appearing under the Concordia imprint. A list of these editions appears as Appendix C, page 181.

Difficulties in establishing correct dates beset any biographer, but writers about Distler, present and future, will be led astray by many sources that should be more accurate. Unfortunately a serious error has been published in one source usually considered nearly infallible in matters musical and Germanic, the encyclopedia *Die Musik in Geschichte und Gegenwart*. According to its biographical sketch of Distler, the composer left Lübeck in 1933 instead of 1937, the year in which he actually moved to Stuttgart. This error has already been copied by two more recent books, one in French and one in Dutch, and will doubtless be perpetuated.

All translations in the present work not otherwise credited are the work of the author. Despite its many shortcomings, it is hoped that this study will shed some light on the life and sacred compositions of a 20th-century master hitherto neglected outside of Germany; if it leads to a further investigation of the music Distler wrote, its purpose will have been realized.

LARRY PALMER

September 15, 1965
Norfolk Division
Virginia State College

NOTE TO PREFACE

1. *Grove's Dictionary of Music and Musicians*, Fifth Edition, ed. Eric Blom (London, 1954), II, 713.

CONTENTS

CHAPTER 1

HUGO DISTLER'S LIFE AND TIMES

Music in Germany at the Beginning of the Twentieth Century

Like the other arts, music shared an interest in the large, the complex, and the colossal in the final days of the 19th century and the early ones of the 20th century, before World War I shook human confidence in everything that had been. Two outstanding composers who might be selected as representative of the colossal transferred to the musical idiom are Richard Strauss (1864—1949) and Gustav Mahler (1860 to 1911), with whose compositions the orchestra reached its utmost limits of size and brilliance.

With Mahler's *Symphony of a Thousand* (No. 8 in E-flat, 1907) and Strauss's monumental tone poems (*Don Juan,* 1888; *Tod und Verklärung,* opus 24; *Ein Heldenleben,* 1898) the Lisztian and Wagnerian influences in German music reached their culmination. Classicism, or at least music of a more "absolute" and less "personal" nature, had been another vital force in the later 19th century — in the music of Brahms (1833—1897), for example, in which Baroque formal patterns were used to such masterful advantage together with the full harmonic palate of the time, or in the complex contrapuntal essays of Max Reger (1873—1916), a composer who might be described as a Baroque master born a century and a half too late.

Strauss's masterful and popular opera *Der Rosenkavalier* dates from 1911; the English author Osbert Sitwell used this music to symbolize the end of an era in his novel *Those Were the Days:*

> That summer, the summer of 1914, it seemed as if the whole of London were a ballroom: (a perpetual three-months-long Waterloo Ball was in progress, and soon all the young people of this perpetual carnival were to be woken to such a sound of

guns — and so insensate a one — as had never shaken the world before . . .)

. . . The dance tunes continued until the end to sound from the windows; fox-trots, tangos, and waltzes. And though that summer the waltzes were fewer in number when compared with other rhythms, nevertheless one of them reigned supreme in every ballroom, the waltz from *Rosenkavalier,* that mocking parody of the old order, that triumph of Ritz-Eighteenth-Century. With its seductive rhythms, its carefully hidden cleverness, it was the last song of an era, and the fox-trots and tangos, of which the elder generation so much disapproved, always made way for it. (Already in Vienna, the home of the waltz, the plot was being prepared by gloved, suave-faced gentlemen in top-hats . . .) But above all the rhythms issuing from so many carnival windows, sounded the voices of the young, joyous and full of confidence; for the last time happy in a sure and stable world. . . . They waltzed on, in complete inexpectation of massacre.[1]

In a real sense this music did mark the end of an era; three years after its composition the most destructive war known until that time was upon the world, and when the fighting ceased four years later, the old order had passed away forever. A new view of history fostered a general new outlook. What was new was not necessarily better than what had been; the influence of musicologists and historians began to be felt, and artists, searching for values to replace the ones lost in the holocaust, looked to the past to gain inspiration for the future.

Among organists a few voices had already called attention to the decadence of the late Romantic instruments, and interest in a return to the organ of the Baroque masters began to grow. Students of Charles-Marie Widor — Emile Rupp and Albert Schweitzer among them — were leaders in the growing awareness that the Romantic organ was not a satisfactory vehicle for the performance of the greatest gems of the organ literature.

The "Orgelbewegung"

With an increased interest in the historical accuracy of musical performances, represented by the scholarly editions of Widor and Schweitzer, the revival of the harpsichord through Wanda Landowska, the builder Pleyel, and Arnold Dolmetsch, and the agitation for a reexamination of the aesthetic and liturgical functions of the organ, it was perhaps a natural solution to turn to the organ of the time when its greatest literature was written. The first contemporary organ to be built according to the specifications of the instruments of the early Baroque era was the so-called "Praetorius" organ built in 1921 for the *Musikwissenschaftliches Institut* in Freiburg by the builder Oscar Walcker through the influence of the musicologist Wilibald Gurlitt. Information for this instrument's specifications and scaling was taken from the second volume of Michael Praetorius' *Syntagma musicum,* the *De organographia* of 1619.[2]

This contemporary organ shared with its older counterparts the distinction of revolutionizing the organ building industry in the succeeding decades; for composers, who were in turn influenced by these instruments, the movement revolutionized organ music as well. This is observable particularly in the works of Johann Nepomuk David, Ernst Pepping, Hugo Distler, and composers who emulated these men.

Shortly after the *Freiburger Musiktage* at which the Praetorius organ was first heard, the distinguished old Scherer-Schnitger organ of the St. Jakobikirche in Hamburg was restored to its 18th-century tonal plan and it, too, was a guide to organists who were attempting to discover what the organ should be and how it could again find its own autonomous spot in the world of music.

Hand in hand with the organ movement came a reexamination of the organ's function in the liturgical church. The organ, as an individual and honorable instrument rather than a synthetic orchestra, sought its rightful place in the liturgy; organists led the fight for the return of the organ to its position as a "preacher in sound," and pastors, too, among them Theodor Kliefoth and Axel Werner Kühl, were influential in this movement.[3]

It was not only the younger generation that benefited by the renewed interest in the authentic organ of the past. Sigfrid Karg-Elert (1877—1933), a minor master of the chorale-prelude form, and a composer in the tradition of Max Reger, showed through his volumes of miniature chorale works that "Germany, if she would but turn her eyes right back to the seventeenth century, was still capable of producing small and beautiful gems."[4] While it is true that Karg-Elert continued to think in terms of the large, Romantic organ, his use of Baroque forms and designs foreshadowed a return to the past as a guide for the future.

The Thomaskantor in Leipzig, Karl Straube (1873—1950), one of the most respected church musicians in Germany, reacted to the vital currents of the age by withdrawing his earlier editions of organ music by the German Baroque masters, published in 1904, and reissuing them in 1926 without the registrations for the "Romantic" organ which he had originally included, hoping thus to correct the wrong ideas of his earlier editions.[5]

A new church music, of which Hugo Distler was to become such an eloquent spokesman, was beginning through the teaching of Straube, Arnold Mendelssohn (1855—1933), and the younger Heinrich Kaminski (1886—1946). Kurt Thomas (b. 1904), only four years older than Distler, studied with these masters; his opus 1, Mass in A Minor, with solo voice, appeared in 1924; together with the works of Johann Nepomuk David and Ernst Pepping, these were the contemporary church music compositions that influenced the young Distler, whose first published works date from 1930.

Gebrauchsmusik and Neoclassicism

Outside the specialized fields of organ and church music, other new forces were at work in Germany. The term *Gebrauchsmusik,* or "music for use," came to be widely used, associated largely with the works of Paul Hindemith (1895—1963). The term denoted mainly music composed for "practical" combinations of instruments, or for whatever instruments happened to be available; it denoted, further, an attempt to "popularize" serious music, in the best sense, and thus to make it available for the majority of the people. This music is "occasional" in that it is composed for specific use and objective in comparison with the subjectivism of the romantic outpouring of soul and self.

The influence of jazz and American popular music was felt in postwar Germany; Kurt Weill (1900—1950) composed his parody of John Gay's *Beggar's Opera, Die Dreigroschenoper,* to a text by Bertolt Brecht in 1929; the following year the same collaborators produced *The Rise and Fall of the City of Mahogonny,* another satiric piece. 1929 was also the year of Hindemith's opera *Neues vom Tage,* a vaudeville with serious and delicately polyphonic music, a great success in its production at the Kroll Theater in Berlin.

Neoclassicism, an attempt to create music that is new in spirit by basing it deliberately on techniques and formal principles of an earlier age, might be better named neo-Baroqueism, or even neo-Renaissanceism. As a style it was arrived at independently by many composers. In one sense it could be considered a natural outgrowth of the *Gebrauchsmusik* principle, for it surely includes a negation of the subjectivism of romantic music, favoring instead a restrained, objective approach to composition with the music itself as primary product rather than a portrait of the composer's soul.

These, then, were the vital currents of German music in the years during which Distler was maturing; out of these many trends, streams, and traditions grew the man Hugo Distler and his music.

Distler's Early Life and Education

Hugo Distler was born in Nuremberg in the German province of Bavaria on June 24, 1908; like St. John the Baptist, on whose feast day his birthday occurred, he was destined to be a "preparer of the way" for the German Lutheran church music of our time, and he was also, like St. John, destined to lose his life in a conflict with the political regime under which he lived.

Not much information is available concerning Distler's early life. He himself was reticent in speaking of these years in Nuremberg. It seems likely that Distler was an illegitimate child; the name Distler came from his mother. His father was probably the owner of a factory. Early in Distler's childhood his mother married another man and emigrated to America. Her parents did not want her to take young Hugo with her; he remained with them in Nuremberg.[6]

A sensitive, nervous, and lonely child living with his grandparents, Distler was not readily understood by them. His first piano lessons began during his early school years at the Privatmusikschule Dupont; despite his obvious musical gifts, he was twice dismissed from this school for disciplinary reasons.[7]

Distler attended the Melanchthon-Gymnasium, from which he was graduated in April 1927.[8] He definitely became interested in the organ during these formative years in the onetime home of Conrad Paumann and Johann Pachelbel! During later years Distler liked to relate how a deacon of the St. Lorenzkirche expelled him from the church for illegal practicing, and how this same deacon apologized in the late 1930s when Distler returned as a well-known artist to play a recital there. Distler later assured the man that he bore him no ill will, since he had only done his duty.

In the fall of 1927 Distler went to Leipzig to begin his studies in the conservatory there. His teachers, among the finest in Germany, were Günther Ramin [9] for virtuose and liturgical organ playing; Hermann Grabner [10] for theory and composition; Carl Adolf Martienssen [11] for piano; and Max Hochkofler, orchestral conducting and score playing.

Hermann Grabner said the following of Distler's career at the Leipzig Conservatory:

> The details put down here concern the student years of Distler, during which I was permitted for a long time to be companion and guide, a directive of fate for which I am unceasingly thankful. It means a special enrichment for a teacher, if, from the great number of students with average talent . . . a young genius suddenly emerges, from whose artistic expressions speaks forth the certainty of a distinguished career, full of blessing for mankind. I had this certainty about Distler from the first instant of our work together. Thus his first work in counterpoint, for which through his former lessons in harmony the best bases had been laid, did not show an everyday mechanical and tiresome solution of the customary practice assignments but rather revealed in every exercise a small work of art, filled with substance and offered with a fascinating ease of execution.
>
> When I spoke above of an "enrichment," it consisted in this case first and foremost in the manner and method by which the spirit of the young creative genius with effortless ease made the traditional rules of art his own and rose above them with an astonishing boldness and independence. The resulting discussions were raised from the sphere of dreary polemics to a higher plane of intellectual clarity, fruitful for teacher and pupil alike. How boring and uninteresting by contrast are "comfortable" students, who perform everything correctly, efficiently, and without contradiction (— not more boring or uninteresting, of course, than "comfortable" teachers, who permit no contradictions and who demand unconditional submission) ![12]

It was Dr. Grabner who steered Distler into the field that was to be his great love as well as the major part of his lifework — church music. At first the young student could not be dissuaded from his preference for the *Kapellmeister* course; he wanted to be a conductor. Grabner eventually was able to persuade Distler that he would still be able to conduct, that his talents would be more suited to church music, and that church music would offer slightly more security.

Security must have been uppermost in the young man's thoughts at this time. He was forced to support himself in Leipzig, and to earn money he worked at copying and reproducing music for a local publisher.

One day he read in the paper that an athletic club in the city needed a choirmaster. He applied for this position and was chosen, at which his predecessor declared war on the new director! Distler told in later years, with high humor, how an escort of bicyclists, members of the club, would come to escort him to rehearsals and home again to protect the slight young man from the persecution of the former leader, a man considerably superior in physical prowess.[13]

Security, or more pressing, the lack of it, was troubling many others throughout the world. On Oct. 24, 1929, the New York stock market crashed, and with it the world's shaky economy. Germany's reviving prosperity, based on American loans, could not survive the withdrawal of these funds and the loss of markets for German manufacturers. Millions in Germany, as elsewhere throughout the world, were unemployed; poverty, rampant hunger, and discontent fostered the rise of National Socialism in Germany. When Chancellor Brüning, in a desperate attempt to improve the moderate majority in the Reichstag, called a general election for Sept. 14, 1930, the Nazis rose from their former 810,000 votes and 12 seats in the Reichstag to 6,409,600 votes, entitling them to 107 seats.

With the Depression deepening everywhere, Distler realized that he would have to seek full-time employment. With heavy heart he explained his impossible economic situation to his teacher Ramin and requested help in finding a position, although he was just beginning the fourth year of his conservatory course.

The recommendations written for Distler by his teachers in Leipzig show the remarkable impression that his talent had made upon them. From Ramin came the following:

> Hugo Distler has been my student in organ for the past three years at this state conservatory. Possessed of a particularly good gift for organ playing, he distinguished himself through a completely extraordinary devotion to his task and devoted industry.

Since he is in addition an artistically independent, sensitive musician, and aware of his artistic gifts, his progress under instruction has always borne the mark of the exceptional. His great gift at composition should also be pointed out, as well as his true inner feeling for church music, which qualifies him for independently artistic performances also in church service playing.

I consider Mr. Distler to be fully qualified to fill a church musician's office to complete satisfaction in each respect — musically, personally, and artistically.

(signed) Günther Ramin
Leipzig, Nov. 2, 1930 [14]

From Hermann Grabner:

Hugo Distler is my student in composition; he has also studied counterpoint with me, and by his great industry and eminent talent he has shown exceptional examples of his abilities. He possesses a highly developed imagination, which enables him to execute successfully great improvisations at the piano and organ. I have no doubt that Mr. Distler will make his way as an artist on the organ and as a composer, and it would please me greatly if he were soon to find a position worthy of his ability.

Leipzig,
Nov. 8, 1930

(signed) Dr. Hermann Grabner
University Music Director [15]

And from Carl Adolf Martienssen:

Mr. Hugo Distler has studied piano with me at the *Landeskonservatorium*. He has attained a respectable mastery so that he will be able to render services of high cultural value also as a pianist and piano teacher. I had the special opportunity to become acquainted with one of his compositions, a large concert sonata for two pianos, which he himself, in cooperation with another student, studied under me for public performance. This performance took place in a public concert of the conservatory and then also on the Leipzig radio, and, to be sure, both times amid expressions of appreciation from the general public and with the highest acknowledgment from professional musicians. I consider Mr. Distler to be the strongest talent in composition to study at the conservatory in recent times. The sonata is masterful in formal design, fresh and full of invention, and highly individual in tonal realization. Moreover, there is in this sonata a purity and a nobility of artistic endeavor and of artistic expression which are rare at the present time.

(signed) Carl Adolf Martienssen
Teacher of piano and head of the
piano classes at the Church Music
Institute in Leipzig.[16]

Meanwhile Ramin had heard of a position for his young student. In September 1930, the 86-year-old Emanuel Kemper announced his retirement as organist of the St. Jakobikirche in the old Hanseatic city of Lübeck. On Oct. 16 Ramin, who knew and prized highly the magnificent old organ of the church, suggested his pupil Walter Tappolet as successor to the aged Kemper. On Oct. 22, however, Tappolet was rejected by the St. Jakobi church council on the grounds that, because of the Depression, only a German citizen could be considered. Tappolet was Swiss. The council requested another recommendation from Ramin.

Evidence that a storm was brewing in Lübeck was apparent when the city's church musicians and private music teachers implored the St. Jakobi council not to bring in an outsider, since the situation economically was already nearly impossible for them.

Ramin next selected Hugo Distler as a candidate for the St. Jakobikirche, and, on Nov. 7, Distler wrote to the pastor and the council concerning the position. Pastor Axel Werner Kühl responded by inviting the young man to come to Lübeck for an audition; meanwhile Distler must have heard about the situation of the music teachers in Lübeck, for he wrote that he would not teach privately, preferring to devote his free time to composition.

On the same date as Distler's letter the council of the St. Jakobikirche passed a resolution instructing these four organists to present themselves for audition: Dähling,[17] Distler, Miss Schneider,[18] and Toppius.[19] The judges were to be Studienrat Grusnick [20] and Studienrat Dr. Jung, while Professor Stahl [21] would also serve as an ex officio member of the church council. On Nov. 20, after a lively debate, the church leaders finally decided to choose the worthiest candidate as proven by the audition, whether that candidate were a native Lübecker or not. The audition was set for the first Sunday in Advent (Nov. 30), and it was further resolved that the judges should not know the order of the contestants until after the playing was finished. The audition for each player was to consist of a chorale with prelude, a fugue from the Bach period, and a free improvisation.

In the final week before the contest the Leipziger Martin Toppius withdrew his application, and these further recommendations were received for Distler:

From the very influential Thomaskantor in Leipzig, Karl Straube:

> Mr. Hugo Distler has urged me to state my views of his talent as a composer. In general, capable and influential judges of talent in Leipzig say that he has strong compositional talent, from whom a notable future is to be awaited.
>
> I am personally familiar with his chorale motet "Herzlich lieb hab' ich dich, o Herr," written for 8-part a cappella choir. In the management of the polyphonic material of absolutely masterful creation, the work impresses through its tightly knit construction and through the richness of its musical content. As soon as it is printed, I shall perform it with the St. Thomas choir. The whole composition is the mature workmanship of a great talent.
>
> If the Jakobikirche selects this artist as its organist, one could only congratulate the congregation on this choice. A musical personality of distinction would then preside at the organ in this church and would, in God-fearing humility, glorify the church service with his noble art.[22]

In addition to the high praise from one of Bach's own successors (two centuries removed, to be sure) at St. Thomas, Martienssen had some private words for the St. Jakobi council:

> If the St. Jakobi Church will permit me, I should like to transmit a private recommendation concerning my pupil Hugo Distler. I would rejoice both personally and artistically if such an eminently talented musician of such a promising future as Mr. Distler were to find with you a position worthy of his talents. I believe that it would be a service to the art of German musical composition to give this young master the grounds for further worthwhile and meaningful creation.[23]

That the choice of a new organist was more than a simple internal matter of concern to the church council is shown by an article which appeared in the *Lübeckische Blätter* for Nov. 23. In it Professor Paul Brockhaus discussed Lübeck's historic significance in the world of sacred music, concluding:

> As is known, the St. Jakobi church fathers (in fortunate possession of one of these old organs, surely the better of the two) are now faced with the filling of the organist's position. It is obvious that (in this choice) the best interests of the congregation must be protected. But this interest may happily be united with the further wishes of the friends of sacred music, if an organist

should be chosen who possesses in addition to his training and qualifications a love and understanding for the churchly duties of his office and also at the same time the gift to create the place in the musical life of our city which belongs especially to the Bach organ of the church and to the other Jakobi organ as well.[24]

After the audition, which took place as scheduled, the church leaders, with Landeskirchenrat Pastor Pautke (of the St. Marienkirche) as chairman, assembled in the sacristy and unanimously selected Candidate I. In the words of Professor Stahl, "The free prelude [on the chorale *Gloria sei dir gesungen*] was the type of superb improvisation which one seldom finds; the Bach D-minor Toccata of faultless technique and lively registration."

The names of the participants were then revealed; number one was Hugo Distler. In spite of the unanimous choice of the judges in his favor and in spite of his superlative references, the council split evenly for Distler and for Dähling, each receiving seven votes.

Two days later the church authorities met for the final decision; discussion availed nothing; neither side would yield in the deadlock. A lot was cast, and the decision fell to Hugo Distler. Thus after every effort and every recommendation, the lot fell to the judges' choice.

From all sides came good news for the young Distler, as his radiant letter to Bruno Grusnick on Dec. 7 shows:

I was very happy to hear the news of my selection. I don't want to omit thanking you heartily for your active interest and help in the difficult competition. I hope confidently that our mutual work together will bear the most beautiful results. . . .

Yesterday I signed my first contract with Breitkopf and Härtel. First, and very soon, my choral motet and Sonata for Two Pianos [25] will be published, perhaps also a Trio for Two Woodwinds and Piano.

I think my first *Abendmusik* should be dedicated to Buxtehude; I mention it, for I hope to be able to count on your choral group for it. I am all anticipation! [26]

The intervening week contained compositional labor, as evidenced by a note to Pastor Kühl, dated Dec. 15:

The promised piano score accompanies this letter, as well as a small cantata to honor the retirement of Mr. Kemper. It would please me greatly if you cared to have your choir perform it; if not complete, perhaps one or more movements from it.[27]

After all the foregoing excitement concerning the choice of a new organist for St. Jakobi, one might expect the traditional "And all lived happily ever after" ending, but all difficulties were not yet resolved. The amount of money available for the organist's salary was impossibly little, consisting of only 59 RM a month, as compared with the prescribed salary for an academically trained church musician — from 780 to 840 RM monthly!

Pastor Kühl exerted every effort to find a larger salary appropriation for his newly appointed organist; a growing concern manifested itself in his letter of Dec. 14 to Günther Ramin, in which he implored Ramin's aid in persuading Distler to take up his duties as of Jan. 1, 1931. The young man had hoped to remain in Leipzig until April 1, so as to receive credit for a complete fourth year of study at the conservatory. Kühl explained that in March the leadership of the provincial church organization divided the leftover funds from the year among the individual congregations. He hoped at this time to receive extra money for the organist, but obviously this would only succeed if the congregation already knew and expressed satisfaction with the new employee.

On the same date Kühl wrote Distler, telling him of the difficulties connected with his selection and instructing him without fail to be in Lübeck to begin his work on Jan. 1.

Distler's sensitive and volatile nature reacted with an indignant letter to the St. Jakobi council.

Leipzig, Dec. 17, 1930

After waiting until this very hour for the official confirmation of my selection and the accompanying contract regulations and conditions, I have just received from Pastor Kühl a communication which definitely forces me to take this position only under very clearly formulated principles and conditions — conditions which, at least to a minimum degree, would perforce insure me a free, unhindered pursuit of my work.

The weighty reason that seems to force me to take this step is the insulting obstinacy of a large number, perhaps the majority, of the church council, with which they — completely contrary to the only criterion I consider valid, the unanimous verdict of all who are expert in these matters and of those who are artistically and church-musically oriented (including both of my fellow contestants) — seek to brand as "irregular" and "unconstitutional" (so

Pastor Kühl reports) an election which for me is unequivocal and, I am convinced, guided by higher Wisdom. And they do this consciously and with means that I must absolutely denounce.

This unobliging, yes, hostile attitude of some of the church leaders forces me to specify the following conditions:

Complete freedom to be responsible for all the affairs concerning the church music of the congregation.

Certainty that there will be regular upkeep on both organs for each church and musical occasion, insofar as the church and its organs are to be used at these functions.

Right to have the nearby organists' house.

Assurance of extra pay for the biweekly, regularly planned evening organ concerts and for taking over of the volunteer church choir.

Certain insurance that, after a quarter year in office, that is, from the first of April on, the salary of 840 RM a year, impossible as a living wage, will be at least doubled.

On my part, I promise to dedicate my full power to work for the musical interests of the congregation. If you should deny me these just conditions or leave me uncertain as to your answer longer than Dec. 24 — an act which, in view of the proximity to Jan. 1, I should have to interpret as a refusal — much as it would pain me, I should have to give up the position once and for all. . . .

(signed) Hugo Distler [28]

Leipzig, C 1, Breitkopfstrasse 26 I

With the help of Ramin's good advice, Pastor Kühl was able to convince Distler that he should begin his office with the new year. What a sensible young man, though, to have written such a letter; considering that he was being forced to leave school for financial reasons, the conditions which he required showed an independent, forceful, and practical spirit!

First Position: Organist at the St. Jakobikirche

And so Hugo Distler began his work as organist of the St. Jakobi Church Jan. 1, 1931. The following six years were to see his development as a performer and the composition of nearly all his sacred works.

The most outstanding and memorable results of the cooperation among Distler, Grusnick, and Pastor Kühl were undoubtedly the 38 musical vesper services presented during Distler's tenure at the church. Pastor Axel Werner Kühl, dynamic young pastor of the church, had been called to serve the St. Jakobi parish in 1928 at the age of 35. He writes in the magazine *Lübeckische Blätter:*

> The plan to institute church services in which the spoken word could be deemphasized to allow the organ, singers, and instruments more independence had already been discussed in the Jakobi congregation for quite some time before Distler came to Lübeck. This expresses the idea that, along with the "Spoken Word" in a narrow sense, there is also a preaching ministry of music.[29]

Not desiring to add to the duties of Distler's elderly predecessor, Pastor Kühl had waited until Kemper's retirement to put his idea into effect. Now the forces were equal to the task, and the first of these Musical Vespers took place on Feb. 15, 1931. The program is representative of the balance between music and word as it evolved in these devotional services.

Organ: Prelude and Fugue in E minor, Buxtehude
Liturgy: Reading of Scripture and Words from Luther
Congregational Chorale: *Erhalt uns, Herr, bei deinem Wort.*
    Text: "In dieser schwer'n, betrübten Zeit"
Choir: "Kyrie," from *Missa Brevis,* Buxtehude
Organ: Two Chorale Fantasies on *Erhalt uns, Herr,* Buxtehude
Choir: Three-voice Canon, *Herr, so du hilfst,* Caldara (1670 to
    1736)
Liturgy: Lord's Prayer and Votum
Choir: Evening Chorale (4-part): Melchior Vulpius, *Hinunter ist
    der Sonnenschein*
Congregational Chorale: *Erhalt uns, Herr.* Text: "Dein Wort ist
    unsers Herzens Trutz"
Organ: Prelude and Fugue in F major, Buxtehude [30]

The next Vespers followed one month later, on March 15; the program consisted of vocal and instrumental compositions of J. S. Bach, the only program among the 38 to present an instrumental composition other than an organ work, the Trio Sonata in D Minor for Two Violins and Organ Continuo.

Doubtless one strong reason for the unity of these services was the participation of both Distler and Pastor Kühl in Grusnick's Lübeck *Sing- und Spielkreis,* the choir employed for most of the services. Pastor and organist were both enthusiastic singers, the pastor, in particular, possessing a fine baritone voice.

On April 17 Distler wrote to Hermann Grabner, "in addition

[to my other duties] I am now cantor of St. Jacobi (the former cantor [Grusnick] having resigned in my favor) : I have two choirs — a volunteer church choir and a boys' choir." [31]

The background for this enlarged scope of activity lies in the impossibility of sustaining life on the organist's salary. Grusnick, with great kindness and understanding, withdrew from his position to allow Distler both salaries, organist's and choirmaster's. Grusnick continued, of course, with his own *Sing- und Spielkreis,* while the volunteer choir was a new venture for Distler's benefit.

This new choir was not, however, a great success, and it remained little more than a valiant attempt. Grusnick had begun the boys' choir; to this tiny group Distler added girls. His group consisted of from 10 to 16 children. This choir served him well, and, grouped about him in a small organ loft, sang often in the morning church services and occasionally in the Vespers. It was for this children's choir that Distler began the chorale settings that developed into the large collection known as *Der Jahrkreis.*

As in the preceding year, Grusnick programed the Heinrich Schütz *St. Matthew Passion* for the Good Friday Vespers (April 3); this music influenced Distler deeply, as we learn from his own words printed in the score of his *Choralpassion,* opus 7. Closely following the Schütz was the next choral Vespers (April 12) with Easter music of Scheidt, Hassler, and Krieger.

The Liturgical Choir of the *Landeskirche,* conducted by Dr. Fritz Jung, sang in the Vespers on May 10; Distler was at the historic small organ. Of lighter substance and great charm was the choral concert of the *Sing- und Spielkreis* on Wednesday, May 20. The choir presented secular songs of the Renaissance, and Distler, besides singing in the group, joined Gertrud Gädecke and Karl Denker, violinists, to perform the Sonata in B-flat for two violins and keyboard by Arcangelo Corelli and the E-major Sonata of Handel.

The fifth Musical Vespers at St. Jakobi took place on June 7, 1931, with the *Sing- und Spielkreis* under Grusnick and Distler at the organ to celebrate the 400th anniversary of the beginning of the Reformation in Lübeck. The music at this program centered about Martin Luther's chorale "Ein feste Burg," with choral settings by Kasper Othmayr and Hans Leo Hassler, and organ preludes by Johann Nicolaus Hanff and Johann Gottfried Walther.

One week later, on June 14, the celebration of the Reformation anniversary was continued on the outdoor stage of the Lübeck city park. This large-scale production marked Distler's first appearance as a composer in his new home city. The composition presented, a *Luther-Cantata,* was scored for singing, speaking, and brass choirs and individual speaking voices. The text was assembled by Paul Brockhaus.

> Orchestra with Women's Chorus: *Aus tiefer Not.* Tune, Wittenberg, 1524
>
> Speech Choir (Men and Women): *Aus der Tiefe rufe ich, Herr, zu Dir* (Ps. 130)
>
> Mixed Choir (5-part): *Aus tiefer Not.* Tune, Strassburg, 1525
>
> Single Voice: *Das Volk, so im Finstern wandelt* (Is. 9:1)
> *Siehe, es kommt die Zeit* (Amos 9:11)
>
> Mixed Choir (4-part) with Winds: *Nun freut euch.* Tune, Wittenberg, 1524
>
> Speech Choir (Women): *Meine Seele erhebet den Herrn*
>
> Mixed Choir (4-part): *Was ich getan hab und gelehrt, das sollst du tun und lehren*
>
> Single Voice: Luther to his beloved Germans
>
> Boys' Choir (3-part): *Ach Gott, vom Himmel sieh darein.* Tune, Erfurt, 1524
>
> Speech Choir (Men): *Ist Gott für uns, wer mag wider uns sein?* (Rom. 8)
>
> Male Choir and Women's Choir, Unison, Antiphonally, with Winds: *Komm, heiliger Geist, Herre Gott.* Tune, Pre-Reformation
>
> Single Voice: *Lutherlied* by Conrad Ferdinand Meyer
>
> Choirs and Congregation (with Winds): *Ein feste Burg.* Tune, Wittenberg, 1529

It is noteworthy that Distler should have been chosen to compose this work rather than the organist of St. Marien, Walter Kraft, who had been in Lübeck since August 1929. A pleased critic mentioned that Distler's chorale settings had "character." [32]

Lübeck did not have long to wait for its next opportunity to hear Distler's compositions. Four days later, on June 18, the choir gallery of St. Katharinen was the setting for a concert by the Lübeck *Sing- und Spielkreis.* Beginning with three 4-part motets of Kurt Thomas, the program continued with Distler's 3-part chorales with ritornelli:

Wir danken dir, Herr Jesu Christ, for women's voices; *Du wunder-grosser Siegesheld,* for mixed chorus; and *Nun bitten wir den heiligen Geist,* again for women's voices. (The last-mentioned was later published in *Der Jahrkreis,* opus 5, as number 22, pp. 38f.)

At this point, the darkness having descended, the candles were lighted; in a setting of contrasts with the crucifix casting its shadow over the singers, the choir continued with Walter Rein's *Ich weiss ein lieblich Engelspiel;* finally, in memory of Grusnick's predecessor at St. Jakobi and the Realschule, Paul Carrière, the *Sing- und Spielkreis* presented Carrière's *Ach bleib mit deiner Gnade* and *Der Mond ist aufgegangen* for unison voices and instruments, and two 4-part chorale settings to original melodies: *Wir danken dir, Gott Vater* and *Da nun der Tag vergangen.*

"Distler's chorales, rich and elegant — works of one with an ability that comes from the deepest passionate inner seed, and an individual spirit that one follows willingly through all its imaginations — held their place with astonishing security next to the creations of the already well-known Kurt Thomas," wrote Leopold Thieme in his review for the *Lübeckische Blätter.*[33]

Distler had reported to Grabner on the musical situation outside the church in Lübeck, relating with fine humor how part of the audience had crept out and part had ostentatiously left the concert hall when the visiting Hamburg Philharmonic had played Stravinsky early in January.

With all his composition, preparing for Vespers and Sunday morning services, was Distler also enjoying social good times and learning to know new friends? Among the singers in Grusnick's *Singkreis* was a lovely girl named Waltraut Thienhaus. She went to the Midsummer Night's festivities with the young composer — the festivities based on the ancient pagan celebration surrounding the natural "mystery" of the shortest night in the year. After this initial fling together, Distler and Miss Thienhaus saw each other only occasionally, for the most part at rehearsals of the *Singkreis.* Then fate, Cupid, or, perhaps, simple economics intervened. Miss Thienhaus' older brother Erich wanted to study organ. He went first to Walter Kraft, the young organist of St. Marien, but Kraft's fee was too high. He began to study with the young Jakobi organist, who did not charge so much; a friendship flourished between the two young men, and Thienhaus invited Distler to his home. It was thus that Distler learned to know the girl whom he was to marry two years later.

Just what further activities filled Distler's first summer in Lübeck has not been recorded. The *Sing- und Spielkreis* presented another evening of choral music *(Chorlieder Abend)* on the outdoor stage of the city park on Aug. 25. Certainly, aside from singing, Distler was composing and practicing!

Regional recognition of Lübeck's importance in the organ world was evident at the *North German Organ Week* in Lübeck in October 1931. At eleven on Saturday morning, October 3, Distler was heard in a demonstration of the "small" St. Jakobi organ. As the central part of the sixth Vespers at the church on the following day, the premiere of Distler's *German Chorale Mass,* opus 3, was sung by the *Singkreis* under Grusnick. All the music that day was by contemporary composers, beginning with *Lydian Toccata* by Engelhard Barthe (born 1906), an organ prelude on *Aus tiefer Not* from Ramin's *Organistenamt,* followed by a choral setting of Kurt Thomas (born 1904). The *German Mass,* Part I, was followed by an antiphonal prelude on the Creed, *Wir glauben all,* by the organist and the chorale sung by the congregation. Then the second part of the Mass, not quite finished as yet; the *Abendmahl* was followed by a repetition of the *Lobgesang,* rather than the *Dankgebet* which eventually formed the last section of the work. A chorale prelude by Karl Hasse (born 1883) and Distler's choral setting of *Nun danket alle Gott,* as well as a *Toccata* for organ by Walter Kraft constituted the remainder of the afternoon's music.

On Monday evening, Oct. 5, Distler's friend and teacher Ramin played a recital on the historic St. Jakobi organ. Sunday, Nov. 1, marked the seventh Vespers, the eighth following it on Nov. 29. That the young man had done a prodigious amount of composing during 1931 could not be disputed, for here, less than two months after the *German Mass,* he offered the first performance of the *Little Advent Music,* opus 4. This work, "little" only in the extent of the forces employed for performance (oboe, violin, flute, organ, 3-part chorus, with narrator and cello as optional participants) is a series of variations on the Luther chorale *Nun komm, der Heiden Heiland.* For this first performance Distler played the keyboard part on the harpsichord, a possibility he suggests in the printed score.[34]

Two days after Christmas, in the ninth musical Vespers, Distler was able at last to present his "Buxtehude-Vesper" which he had mentioned to Grusnick in the letter dated more than a year previous (see page 23). Such Buxtehude favorites as the organ fantasy *Wie schön leuchtet der Morgenstern* and the Prelude and Fugue in A Minor, the solo cantatas *Lobet, Christen, euren Heiland* and *Singet dem Herrn ein neues Lied,* and the 5-part *Magnificat* with strings and continuo were on this Christmas program.

Just how much a part of the Lübeck tradition Distler felt himself at the end of this first work-filled year may be summed up in this letter to Waldemar Klink: [35]

> I also believe that first of all the Lübeck "younger set" (among whom I count the only slightly older organist of St. Marien, Walter Kraft, and the Buxtehude researcher and scholar, Bruno Grusnick, and to whom I, although originally a Leipziger, seem to belong) are consistent and even prejudiced, if you will, in their enthusiasm for the music from the 16th century, back to the old French (Machaut), English (Madrigalists), and Netherlanders of the early school (Okeghem), and in their endeavors to make this music, and only this music, the basis for their own.
>
> We have the most priceless treasures from this period (I myself a 3-manual, 30-rank organ from the years 1496 to 1600, in St. Marien the equally old and beautiful *Totentanz* organ), which for us signify life present and future.[36]

The new year, 1932, was not a happy one insofar as Germany was concerned. The Depression was at its worst; five million workers had no work; political intrigue, counterintrigue, and counter-counter-intrigue was rife. And it was bitterly cold; blizzards, swept by freezing winds, lashed the land; the Baltic was frozen for miles, as far as the eye could see and farther.

In Lübeck distinguished music-making continued. Distler presented his children's choir for the first time in Vespers, his 10th at St. Jakobi, on Jan. 24. The choir sang three 2-part songs by Kaspar Othmayr: *Ach Gott, vom Himmel sieh darein; Wär' Gott nicht bei uns diese Zeit;* and *Herr Christ, der einig Gotts Sohn.* For a second group the choir sang three 3-part compositions by its choirmaster: *Nun bitten wir den heiligen Geist* (later published in *Der Jahrkreis,* No. 22); *In Gottes Namen fahren wir* (*Jahrkreis,* 42); and *Vater unser im Himmelreich* (*Jahrkreis,* 49).

On Feb. 7 Grusnick and the *Spielkreis* journeyed to Schlutup to present a sacred concert in the St. Andreas Church there. Distler played music of Sweelinck, Pachelbel, and Buxtehude, and the choir sang Vulpius, Bach, and Buxtehude.

The 11th Musical Vespers was heard in St. Jakobi on Feb. 21; the 12th on March 25 was the now traditional Good Friday singing of the Schütz *St. Matthew Passion.* Around this masterwork Distler worked the three great Kyrie chorale preludes from the Bach *German Organ Mass* (*Klavierübung,* Part III).

During the early spring Distler purchased his large concert harpsichord from Neuport, the noted German builder; he also organized the Lübeck Chamber Orchestra, which gave its first public concert on April 23 in the Logensaal on the St. Annenstrasse. There were nine players in the chamber group: Gertrud Gädeke, Maria Mahlau, Concertmaster H. Millies, and Hermann Talman, violins; Karl Denker, viola; Leopold Thieme, Gerhard Berg, and Dr. Julius Paulsen, celli; Walter Metelmann, contrabass; Distler conducted from the harpsichord. The program consisted of Franz Xaver Richter's *Sinfonia da Camera;* solo harpsichord music of Handel — the Eighth Suite (F minor), the Chaconne in G Major; the Stamitz Sonata in G for Violoncello and Harpsichord, and the Karl Philipp Emanuel Bach Concerto in D Minor for Harpsichord and Strings.

The reviewer of this concert for the *Lübeckische Blätter,* J. Hennings, had only words of praise for Hugo Distler. While commenting that the group still had problems of intonation, balance, and exactness of ensemble, Hennings stated that Distler would soon reach anything he had set himself as a goal, and he continued, "The best of the evening came from Hugo Distler — the Handel Eighth Suite, one of the most beautiful of a whole group; and the lively G-major Chaconne, musically and technically on such a high plane that the listeners were unwilling to let the artist go." [37]

The very next afternoon there followed another Vespers at Saint Jakobi, in which Distler performed two mighty Bach works, the *Allein Gott* trio (Leipzig *Great Eighteen* Chorale Preludes) and the Toccata, Adagio (listed on the program as "Largo"), and Fugue in C Major.

On Thursday another of Distler's groups performed; this, the DHB choir *(Deutsche Hilfe Band),* sang a program of "old secular folk music from the 16th and 17th centuries." The choral settings, all by Distler, reveal the side of his compositional talent that was to culminate in the jocund *Neues Chorliederbuch* and *Mörike-Chorliederbuch* of the late 30s. On the program were settings of *Wach auf, meins Herzens Schöne* (variations for mixed chorus and instruments); *Hab mein Wagen vollgeladen* (men); *Der Mond ist aufgegangen* (unison women's voices with instruments); *Innsbruck, ich muss dich lassen* (mixed chorus); and two sets of variations for chorus with instruments: *Mir ist ein feins brauns Maidelein* and *Wo soll ich mich hinkehren* (later published by Bärenreiter, No. 2046). To these offerings were added instrumental works, with Distler at the harpsichord; Sonata IV in D for Violin and Cembalo, Handel; Sonata in D Minor for Two Violins and Continuo, J. S. Bach; and the Incidental Music to an English tragedy *Abdelazer* by Purcell. The program stated that the choir had a rehearsal each Wednesday evening in the DHB House, Hürterdamm 18, in Lübeck.

The 14th Vespers at St. Jakobi, May 29, featured the *Singkreis* in works of Heinrich Schütz and settings of *Nun bitten wir den heiligen Geist* by Distler. Two familiar organ works framed the service: the Bach Toccata and Fugue in D Minor and Buxtehude's Prelude, Fugue, and Chaconne in C.

The political maneuvers that were ripping the Weimar Republic to shreds were continuing at a furious rate. Franz von Papen, of whom it was said that neither his friends nor his enemies took him seriously, was named Chancellor of the Republic on June 1. To attain this position he had made a deal with the Nazis, whom he then promptly rewarded by lifting the ban on the Nazi riot squads, the so-called S. A. *(Sturm-Abteilung)* on June 15. Political violence and murder swept the land. Between June 1 and 20 in Prussia alone there were 461 pitched battles, costing 82 lives and wounding more than 400. Closer to Lübeck, in Hamburg's residential suburb of Altona, 19 persons were killed and 285 wounded during a Nazi parade on July 17.

Lübeck again played host for the *Orgeltage,* July 28 to Aug. 7. Four names, all famous in retrospect, highlighted the 1932 event: Fritz Heitmann, who played the Bach *Klavierübung,* Part III, on the great organ at St. Marien; Walter Kraft, performing hitherto unknown organ works of Buxtehude on the *Totentanz* organ at the same church; Günther Ramin, with works of early German masters at the small

St. Jakobi organ; and Hugo Distler, who conducted a chamber concert in the St. Annenkloster, Lübeck's museum for medieval treasures.

For this concert Distler played Bach's fifth French Suite, the E-minor Toccata, and conducted the D-minor Concerto for Harpsichord and Strings, as well as the Handel Concerto Grosso No. 7, from the harpsichord. This performance was reviewed in the national church music magazine *Musik und Kirche,* and it is refreshing to note that Distler's efforts here were not completely successful! There were, seemingly, grave ensemble and rhythmic problems, although the performance was a "lively" one.[38]

Far more successful for the young composer was the *Geistliche Abendmusik* on Sunday, Oct. 23, in St. Katharinen. The program, entirely of Distler's compositions, was especially noteworthy as it included the first performance of the completed *German Chorale Mass,* opus 3, which had been performed unfinished the preceding year (Oct. 4, 1931). The program opened with two stanzas of the evening hymn *Christ, der du bist der helle Tag;* then the children's choir from St. Jakobi sang three free motets from the *Jahrkreis: Herr, schicke was du willst* (No. 50); *Der Mensch, vom Weibe geboren* (No. 36); and *Gott ist unsere Zuversicht* (No. 31). Following the *Choralmesse,* sung by the *Singkreis* and conducted by Grusnick, the children sang three more chorale motets from the *Jahrkreis: Wir danken dir, Herr Jesu Christ; Allein Gott in der Höh' sei Ehr';* and *Vater unser im Himmelreich.* The concert closed with stanzas three and four of the opening chorale.

On Nov. 6, the day of the year's fourth national election (in which the Nazis lost two million votes and 34 seats in the Reichstag), Hans Meyer of Berlin joined the Lübeckers for the 15th Vespers at St. Jakobi. As a tribute to Schütz, who died on Nov. 6, 1672, the vocal music was all from his pen, including the chorales and the *Amen.* The soloist was heard in three of the *Kleine geistliche Konzerte,* the choir in the "Kyrie" from the *German Mass* and the 6-part motet *Die Himmel erzählen.* The organ music was by Pachelbel.

Music in St. Jakobi continued as the year drew to a close; an enacted Dance of Death of Nov. 16 used the music of Leonhard Lechner and probably provided the germ that grew into Distler's own *Totentanz* motet the following year. The 16th and 17th Vespers brought this series to the new year; the former provided an Advent program of music and word similar to Distler's opus 4, which had been heard the preceding year, but using compositions on *Nun komm, der Heiden Heiland* by various composers — Resinarius, Othmayr, Osiander, Praetorius, and Hassler. Vespers 17 is of interest for the small notice at the foot of the program, announcing that the church was heated — the first time such a notice had been included. Musically the program offered Renaissance choral music, Baroque organ music, and the first performance of Distler's own Partita for Organ, *Nun komm, der Heiden Heiland.*

Two other concerts featured Distler in one capacity or another. He joined the young Leipzig pianist Karl Seeman in a program of two-piano music under the auspices of the *Deutsche Bühnengemeinde.* The duo performed Christoph Bach's Sonata in G, the Mozart D-major Sonata; Schumann's Andante with Variations, and Brahms' F-minor Sonata, transcribed by the composer from the original string quintet.

Finally, Distler was at the organ in St. Jakobi for a concert of "old Christmas music" (Sunday, Dec. 11). This program included much interesting music such as four movements from a hypomixolydian mass of Lassus and the Dufay Gloria *(ad modum Tubae).*

Because of the following comments by Hennings in the *Lübekkische Blätter,* relations with Walter Kraft may have been a little strained at this time.

> The works of two young Lübeck church musicians, Walter Kraft and Hugo Distler, were heard in the sacred concert. For me there can be no doubt that the St. Jakobi organist is, musically speaking, the deeper personality — not only the more mature but also the more enlightened. Hugo Distler always surprises a person anew with the accuracy of his musical language, a language no longer committed to groping about for the proper expression but already master of it with a sovereignty that is all but amazing for the composer's youth. Additional features of his style, important to him as a church musician, are the religious fervor of his expression, the deep conviction of the holiness of God's Word, and the warmth of feeling elicited by this conviction. This warmth makes itself felt again and again, and one is transported as a result.[39]

Two more of Distler's works were published during 1932 by Breitkopf and Härtel, the last of Distler's dealings with this firm.

They were the *Choralmesse,* opus 3, and the *Kleine Adventsmusik,* opus 4. Beyond the vast loads of composition and the proof correcting involved in these new publications, the composer was also occupied during these closing months of 1932 on the *Choralpassion* (published as opus 7), the postscript to which is dated December 1932.

On Jan. 30, 1933, President Hindenburg named the "Austrian Corporal" chancellor, though he had previously vowed that he would never be chancellor of the German Republic. In a sense he was right, for with the appointment of Adolf Hitler, the doom of the Republic was sealed; Germany's rendezvous with her bitter destiny moved nearer.

For Distler 1933 was an eventful year, the year of his marriage and also of his first contracts with the Bärenreiter publishing firm. His position at St. Jakobi became more or less full-time, regarding salary, and Distler accepted the extra duties of two three-day visits monthly to Spandau, a suburb of Berlin, where he taught composition and theory in the Johannesstift. His regular work continued; the 18th Vespers was scheduled for Feb. 26 and featured contemporary church music: works by Kraft, Carrière, and Kurt Thomas and the first performance of Distler's own *Kleine geistliche Abendmusik* for 3-part choir, two obbligato instruments, and cembalo — a "rondo-cantata" based on the chorale *Christ, der du bist der helle Tag.*

The Nazi terror, more or less legalized now that Hitler was chancellor, was first felt in the musical life of Germany on March 11, when Carl Ebert and Fritz Stiedry, director and conductor, respectively, of the Berlin Civic Opera were dismissed from their posts for not meeting the Aryan paragraph of the Nazi statutes.[40]

The following day, March 12, was designated throughout the nation as *Volkstrauertag* (Day of National Mourning, similar to our Memorial Day). In the 19th Vespers at St. Jakobi the *Singkreis* offered works of a memorial nature by Heinrich Schütz, and Distler played Buxtehude's E-minor Chaconne, Prelude and Fugue in G Minor, and the Sweelinck Variations on *Mein junges Leben hat ein End'.*

During these busy winter months Distler had been coaching Heinz Marten and Paul Gümmer, who were to be soloists in the premiere of his *Choralpassion,* opus 7. Gümmer, with whom Distler studied voice,[41] related how Distler worked very hard to instill the proper sense of freedom in the Schütz-styled unaccompanied solo recitatives. The first performance of the *Passion* was sung by the Berlin Bach Chorus, conducted by Professor Wolfgang Reimann, on March 19.

The work was heard in Lübeck on the successive evenings of Monday and Tuesday, April 3 and 4, with choirs made up from the choir of St. Marien, the association for church choir singing, the Lübeck *Sing- und Spielkreis,* and the St. Jakobi choirs. Walter Kraft conducted the choir that sang the Passion narrative; and Hermann Fey directed the chorale choir. Soloists were Prof. Dr. Hans Hoffmann from Halle and, again, Paul Gümmer from Hannover. Distler, at the historic organ, introduced the programs with his organ partita on *Jesus Christus, unser Heiland.* (Published in opus 8/III)

The *Choralpassion* was the first of Distler's works to receive true national recognition; the members of the *Arbeitsgemeinschaft zur Pflege und Förderung zeitgenössischer evangelischer Kirchenmusik* received copies of the score as a music bonus for 1933, and already in that first year the work had more than a dozen performances throughout the land, including those in Leipzig (Straube), Barmen (Grote), Nuremberg (Klink), Kassel (Stürmer), and in both Königsberg and Frankfurt-am-Main, conducted by Geiss.[42]

The 20th Vespers at St. Jakobi April 14 was concerned with the Schütz *St. Matthew Passion* again.

Fifty-two 3-part chorale settings, many of which had been used for the children's choir at St. Jakobi (in some Distler himself sang the baritone part) were readied for publication under the title *Der Jahrkreis* ("The Year's Cycle"), opus 5. The collection, dedicated to the St. Jakobi pastor, Axel Werner Kühl, was Distler's first Bärenreiter publication. Hereafter all his works were issued by this company.

On Friday, April 28, the *Singkreis,* Distler, and some of his organ pupils presented a special *Geistliche Abendmusik* to aid the fund for unemployed young people. Jan Bender played the prelude, Buxtehude's Prelude, Fugue, and Chaconne in C. The choir sang two motets by Schütz; Käte Derlien played the Scheidt fantasy *Ich ruf' zu Dir.* The youth choir sang two Distler settings, *Herr Gott, dich loben wir* and *Erstanden ist der Herre Christ;* the remainder of the program consisted of works by Buxtehude: the cantata *Jesu, meine Freude,*

Distler's playing of the Prelude and Fugue in G Minor, and the cantata *Befiehl dem Engel, dass er komm.*

The government commissioner for Lübeck seemingly was in communication with Distler at this time concerning a concert organ for the city for in an extant first draft of a letter dated May 20, 1933, Distler writes, "The idea of a *concert organ* does not exist for me — only the church organ." [43]

At this same time plans were being made to set up a national conservatory in Lübeck. Frau Distler told the author the story of how Distler was asked to cooperate in setting up a plan of instruction for the new institution. He wrote in very strong terms to the commissioner, terms that were not politic, presumably. Impetuously, as was his nature, he posted the letter, then began to have qualms about the language he had used. There was no way to recover the document from the postbox, but the young man was fortunately able to intercept it by appearing at the commissioner's home just as the mail was being delivered and convincing the rather stupid housemaid that he should be given the letter.

The 21st Vespers was an event of May 21st, with works of Pachelbel, Buxtehude, and Bach. Elsewhere others were having problems with National Socialism. In Berlin Arnold Schoenberg and Franz Schrecker were dismissed from the faculty of the Prussian Academy of Arts because of racial impurity.[44]

Further attesting to Distler's widening fame was his selection to be guest contemporary composer at the *Kirchengesangstage* in Stuttgart, June 10—12. Here Distler rehearsed the choral ensemble and conducted it at the festival service in his motets *Lobe den Herren* and *Es ist das Heil;* this music was heard just before Oskar Söhngen's address *Contemporary Church Music and the Evangelical Church.*

Back in Lübeck preparations were in full swing for the *Orgeltage* scheduled for June 28—30. Features included recitals by Ramin at St. Marien on the *Totentanz* organ and by Distler at St. Jakobi.

Other commitments for the summer are not recorded; the greatest preparation, however, must have been occasioned by Distler's forthcoming marriage to Waltraut Thienhaus, an event of Oct. 14, in the St. Jakobi church.

The 22d Vespers, Nov. 5, featured the only appearance at these services of antiphonal psalmody between pastor and choir. All the vocal compositions and arrangements were by Distler. The service was framed by the *Klavierübung,* Part III, prelude and postlude, Bach's monumental E-flat Prelude and Fugue. The congregation sang two stanzas of the chorale *Lobe den Herren,* between which the choir sang Distler's motet on this tune.

The choral antiphon, God Is Our Shield, prefaced the alternating psalmodic recitation of Rom. 8:31, 33, 35, 38-39; after which the antiphon was repeated. Following another antiphon, To God Be Praise and Honor, the pastor and choir alternated the verses of the Magnificat.

The first performance of Distler's opus 10 was only a partial one: the opening chorus and the chorale variations on *Es ist ein Ros' entsprungen* from *Die Weihnachtsgeschichte* were sung at a program of Christmas music in the St. Aegidien church on Dec. 17. The first Lübeck performance of the complete work was an event of Dec. 26, the 23d Vespers at St. Jakobi.

The thoroughly delighted critic praised the newest work from the master in the most glowing terms, and his review elicited this very instructive letter from Pastor Kühl, dated Dec. 27:

> Please permit me, before I depart for a church conference, to do something I would otherwise have preferred to do personally: express my special thanks for the fine mention of our singing [Kühl also sang in the *Singkreis*] and of Distler's compositions in St. Aegidien, and for the announcement of our Christmas Vespers yesterday. It pleases us very much, naturally, when our undertakings are supported by professional critics. Please do not be surprised that I make such an expression my affair. It is through this fantastic working partnership among us three — certainly something completely extraordinary and not often found — that support for one of us is at the same time help for the others. Moreover, I believe a good portion of the excellent success of our Vespers must be credited to this working partnership, this working together of altar, choir, and organ. Laymen, too, will notice this clearly through the participation of the pastor and organist-composer in the *Singkreis* there in the choir gallery.
>
> The *Singkreis* with its human common interest is the ever new source of power for our work in the field of church music, and the basis for our "congregational music" in the best sense of the word. Grusnick understands masterfully how to arouse and hold the joy of singing. Again yesterday we had to marvel at him. Because of the absence of several voices the tenor was not as

strong as it should have been. So Grusnick sang the entire tenor part along with the chorus, as well as the solo Evangelist's part. When you add to this his chief work, conducting the choir, you have a truly unique accomplishment.

So far as Distler's wonderful composition is concerned, I should like to give expression to my great joy over the statement in your review that the parts sung in St. Aegidien impressed you with their simplicity. The impression Distler makes, I think, is more and more "popular" in the best sense [i. e., of the people]. For me the curious thing about all this is (as you may have seen by looking at the score subsequently) that in general the performance can be carried off successfully only by an especially well-trained choir. The unequal barring in the various parts, the changing rhythm of the individual voices, and the difficulty of the entrances certainly make heavy demands, it seems to me. That in spite of these the music is so extraordinarily and strongly effective, therein lies the special secret of Distler's art. To me personally the places where this young man allows the basic power of religion to break forth are always particularly worthwhile. But this goes further than it should in a letter meant as an expression of heartfelt thanks to you. I should enjoy speaking with you personally about this matter sometime.[45]

The yearly *Volkstrauertag* occurred in 1934 on Feb. 25. It was marked by the 24th Musical Vespers at St. Jakobi. The major music consisted of Leonhard Lechner's *Deutsche Sprüche von Leben und Tod*. Thematic organ music included Pachelbel's *Wenn mein Stündlein vorhanden ist* and the Sweelinck *Mein junges Leben hat ein End*.

The 25th Vespers took place on Good Friday, March 30, with the *St. Matthew Passion* of Schütz and J. S. Bach's organ prelude *Herzlich tut mich verlangen,* erroneously ascribed to the *Orgelbüchlein* collection, on the program; also heard was the simple G-minor Fantasia of Pachelbel.

That music was to be made a weapon in the propaganda of the third Reich had been clearly indicated the preceding November with the organization of the *Reichsmusikkammer*. The order issuing from this headquarters on April 22 decreed that all German singing societies were to be amalgamated into one large national *Sängerbund* in conformity with the Nazi principle of leadership.

The 26th Vespers at St. Jakobi was scheduled for Cantate Sunday, April 29. Opening with the sparkling D-major Prelude and Fugue of Buxtehude, the program continued with Distler's chorale motet

Lobe den Herren (opus 6/II), as well as the first performance of the rhythmically arresting motet, *Singet dem Herrn ein neues Lied,* published as number one of the series *Geistliche Chormusik,* opus 12, originally planned to include 52 compositions, one for each Sunday of the church year. The pastor and congregation alternated verses in the Te Deum, and the Vespers concluded with the Prelude and Fugue in C Major of J. S. Bach.

A candlelit church was the setting for Distler's organ recital at St. Jakobi on Tuesday, May 8, at 9:45 in the evening. The capacity audience could "imagine itself back in the time of Lübeck, Buxtehude, and Bach, from each of whom Distler played a Prelude and Fugue (Lübeck, E-major; Buxtehude, D-major; and Bach, C-major) with careful, masterly hand and with loving penetration of the style," as one newspaper account described the recital.[46]

There was much local fanfare over the world premiere of Distler's secular cantata *Ewiges Deutschland* (Eternal Germany), an event of May 24, 1934, in the city theatre. Despite the propaganda, the work was not very successful and has disappeared from all notice, score and all, except for a few yellowing newspaper accounts. The text by Wolfram Brockmeier was set as five short a cappella choruses and as melodramatic recitation. In form, the work consisted of an introduction, fanfare, intermezzi (all orchestral), and eight individual and group dances, conceived as rhythmical chamberworks.

These dances, or dance-tableaux, were titled *Liebliche Gefährtin* (Lovely Companioness), conceived after old minuets; *Lauschendes Mädchen* (Eavesdropping Girl), containing a "longing motive"; two tone-paintings, *Gang zum Dom* (Procession to the Cathedral) and *Trauernde Frau* (Sorrowing Woman); *Fröhlicher Maigang* (Happy Journey in May) and *Nürnberger Sommertag* (Summer Day in Nuremberg) — these folkdances designed from old woodcuts; *Wandlung* (Transformation), a "will-o'-the-wisp" dance; and, finally, *Aussaat.* (Seed Sowing)

The music critic who reviewed the performance was complimentary enough to please the propagandists but expressed unhappiness over the orchestral writing. He found the instrumentation severe and thought that, "in spite of the exciting rhythms, the work seemed somewhat too monotonous, with not enough profile and substance." [47]

This criticism interests in the light of Distler's overall avoidance of large orchestral ensembles in his subsequent works. Frau Distler maintained that her husband always hoped to write more for orchestra but felt uncomfortable in this medium, a feeling that might be traced back to his Leipzig training; Professor Grabner also felt uneasy in composing for the orchestra and thus was unable to transmit much feeling for orchestration to his students in composition.[48]

Back on more familiar ground, with works of Pachelbel, Schütz, and Bach, the 27th Musical Vespers took place on Sunday, June 3. Also in St. Jakobi, on June 19, was heard one of the first programs of the new Lübeck *Staatskonservatorium und Hochschule für Musik,* where Distler was teacher of organ and head of the church music department. With Professor Irmgard Reimann from Berlin as soloist, Distler at the organ, Hans Millies, violinist, and Jan Bender at the harpsichord, the following program of compositions by J. S. Bach was performed:

Organ: Fantasie and Fugue in C Minor
Three Songs from *Schemelli's Gesangbuch*
Organ: Trio Sonata in G Major
Recitative and Aria for Alto, Cantata 148
    So wie der Hirsch nach frischem Wasser schreit
Organ: Three Organ Chorales
    Allein Gott (trio)
    Das alte Jahr (melismatic, *Orgelbüchlein*)
    Der Tag, der ist so freudenreich (c. f. in soprano, *Orgel-
    büchlein*)
Aria from Cantata 11
    Ach, bleibe doch, mein liebstes Leben
Organ: Prelude and Fugue in C Major

In the summer of 1934, for the first vacation since their marriage, Distler and his wife traveled to Berlin, where Distler played an organ recital on the priceless Arp Schnitger organ in the Charlottenburg Palace in July; then on, for a real vacation and rest, to Mittenwald in Bavaria, between Barmsee and Garmisch. Here, in the quiet and seclusion he loved so well, surrounded by mountain scenery so beautiful that it could not fail to inspire one, Distler worked on his secular oratorio to a text by Schiller, *Das Lied von der Glocke.* (The Song of the Bell)

Since Distler composed at the keyboard and since the small inn where the couple was staying did not have a piano, he had to go quite some distance, about a half-hour's quick walk, to a small house where there was an instrument. Frau Distler, recalling this first summer vacation, remembered one humorous occasion when her husband, caught in a hailstorm as he began the homeward walk from his "composing-house," had to run the whole way, arriving at the inn completely drenched, breathless but happy.

One of the most personal contemporary articles concerning Distler was the work of Dr. Fritz Stege, a music critic from Kassel. Dr. Stege, in Lübeck to attend the premiere of a now forgotten operetta (*Die Liebesnächte* by Schielderup), found that he had an hour to fill before curtain time. Deciding to visit Hugo Distler, he strolled to the St. Jakobi church, where he heard organ music. He called up to the organ loft, found that it was indeed the young organist who was practicing, and was soon invited to come into the organist's home, the old brick dwelling only a few steps away across the churchyard. In Dr. Stege's words,

> . . . And then I seated myself in the tiny, tasteful organists' house, with its authentic country furniture. Across from me a blond, northern type, quiet and simple, a dreamy look in the intelligent eyes, and so young . . .
> "How old are you really?" I could not resist asking.
> "Twenty-six," was the answer.
> With gentle voice he recounted bits of his life story. "I was educated in a strict religious school [Melanchthon-Gymnasium, Nuremberg] . . ." His well-thought-out words were based on the foundation of a deep seriousness concerning life. He is not one of those who takes life lightly — and even less lightly his art, for each signifies the same thing for him.

Dr. Stege asked the young man about the progress of his career and heard from Distler's lips of his forthcoming plans: a performance in the near future of the *Totentanz*, a new motet; a contract received from the State Radio in Hamburg for the composition based on Schiller's *Das Lied von der Glocke* [see page 42]; his hopes soon to compose a singspiel based on the story of Tyll Eulenspiegel [never realized]; how he had just been named head of the church music department at the Lübeck *Staatskonservatorium*. The article continues,

> We spoke together concerning the pressing questions of our time, of a "popular" music, of the choral-music movement.

Distler had sound observations and was informed about all actual questions, although personally he remains far away from all the action in this cultural fighting.

". . . I am glad that I don't live in a large city, not in Berlin," he looked at me rather uncertainly, to see if I were vexed — no, most certainly not, dear contemporary master!

". . . Far from confusion, to create in silence, that is my work . . ."

To be sure, great works mature only in silence, and yet I expressed surprise that his works were not more often heard in prominent places, as at composer's festivals.

"Yes, I am completely uninformed about getting works programed at such places. Couldn't you tell me more about this?"

Then Distler proceeded, "I am convinced that a foundation for our musical life can only be based successfully on singing, on choral music."

What followed next was largely propaganda for the benefit of the *Reichsmusikkammer.* The two men discussed the increasing popularity of folk instruments, such as the harmonica. Distler mentioned his own short motet *Lobe den Herren,* useful and practical for even the smallest choirs, as a contribution to this new "popular" music.

Distler's words sounded natural and unforced. He dismissed the knottiest problems with a wave of his hands, as, for example, when I questioned him concerning his position in regard to the Organ Renaissance *(Orgelbewegung).* Here he shared my view that truly historic instruments belong to, indeed, are nearly required for, a stylistically exact performance of the preclassic masters. But then he said, "The *Orgelbewegung* must be based on the church. Its renewing can only succeed when it comes from the Christian spirit." And this sentence stood as his mandate, firm as one of the walls of the room. There was nothing to clarify, nothing to expand.

After a few minutes more, Dr. Stege took his leave, "convinced that this young, quiet, mature man and the lovely, dreamlike northern city Lübeck, city of churches, together formed a deep-seated artistic unity." [49]

It was becoming more difficult to create, or do anything else artistic, in silence; the official madness of the *Musikkammer* reached ever more deeply into artistic affairs, both personal and public. The government decreed on Sept. 29 that artists and musicians were no longer permitted to use foreign-sounding names; Oct. 31 was the final date for changing such names back to the homey, Aryan, originals. Further, the Nazi *Kulturgemeinde* commissioned both Rudolf Wagner-Regeny and Julius Weismann to write new musical settings of *A Midsummer Night's Dream* to replace those of Mendelssohn, inadmissable to the Third Reich because of the composer's race.[50]

In Lübeck, however, away from this nonsense, the choir gallery of the Katharinenkirche was the setting for the world premiere of Distler's *Lübecker Totentanz,* better known simply as the *Totentanz* (Dance of Death). The northern city has been identified with this theme since an unknown medieval master painted, in a side-chapel of the Marienkirche in 1463, the well-known pictures of death's invitations to high and lowly to come to the final dance with him. The famous small "Buxtehude" organ of the church was known by the name *Totentanz* organ because of its proximity to these paintings. And now, continuing this heritage from his adopted city, Distler had composed, to a text by the local Johannes Klöcking, a motet consisting of short choral settings, interspersed with the spoken dialogs of Death and his victims, from Kaiser to Infant. The first performance of this gripping work was on Sept. 29; the *Singkreis,* conducted by Bruno Grusnick, and members of the *Dramatischer Laienchor* (for the spoken parts) participated in the premiere.

It was a busy season that began so auspiciously for Distler! In addition to his teaching duties in Lübeck were the commitments he filled in the conservatory in Berlin's suburb of Spandau, to which he commuted weekly during the remaining years of his stay in Lübeck. And there were family matters to be thought of during this autumn, for the first child of Hugo and Waltraut Distler was born Dec. 5 and baptized Barbara.

With Barbara's advent came also the problem of a suitable home. The young couple had continued to live in the traditional organists' house, provided for Distler by St. Jakobi, located only a few steps from the church door. But this dwelling, charming and historic though it was, had certain drawbacks: a persistent bad odor, no bathroom, and only four small rooms above the first floor. The Distlers felt that it was not the proper environment for their firstborn, so the family moved, lock, stock, and Neupert harpsichord, to live with Waltraut's grandmother at No. 4 Falkenstrasse. Here they stayed for half a year; a further move took them out to the edge of Lübeck's inner city to the home of Frau Distler's parents, the Thienhaus villa. The Distler family occupied the upper floor of this house at 21 Ellsässerstrasse from 1935 until the departure from Lübeck in 1937.

The first Musical Vespers of this season was rather late in the schedule as compared with other years; No. 28 in the whole series, it occurred on Jan. 6, 1935, and consisted of the Distler *Weihnachtsgeschichte,* opus 10.[51]

At a chamber music program consisting of compositions by Bach and Handel, a new dimension was added to Distler's performing: the use of a pedal harpsichord. The date was Sunday, April 7, 1935, and the program included the *Italian Concerto* for harpsichord and the organ Prelude, "Largo" [sic], and Fugue in C Major, as well as two German arias by Handel for soprano, violin, and harpsichord, and the Handel E-major Sonata for violin and harpsichord. The performers, in addition to Distler, were Margarete Burren, soprano, and Bruno Rahlf, violin.

Vespers 29 fell on Good Friday, April 19, 1935; as usual, it consisted of the Schütz *St. Matthew Passion.*[52]

Late in the spring Distler made a trip to Dresden at the invitation of the cantor of the Sophienkirche. Hans Heintze, the newly appointed organist and cantor, had instituted a regular series of *Abendmusiken* to bring the Silbermann organ into prominence; J. S. Bach's son Friedemann had at one time been organist of this church for 14 years, but since his time the organ had been rather neglected. Distler's concert was the final one before summer vacation; he played the Buxtehude Prelude and Fugue in G Minor, a Bach trio sonata, three organ chorales, and the Prelude and Fugue in C: with Heintze conducting, the choir of the church sang Distler's *Choralmesse,* opus 3, and at the conclusion of the concert the composer played his *Nun komm, der Heiden Heiland* partita.[53]

Under the auspices of the *Arbeitskreis für Hausmusik,* a church music conference took place in Kiedrich im Rheingau on Sunday, May 12. At eleven the town's main organ was demonstrated by Distler; and at 2:30 a choral Vespers was scheduled, for which Distler performed old organ music of the 16th and 17th centuries.

The Lübeck *Orgeltage* for 1935 were August 2 and 3. Fritz Heitmann was again a featured artist, playing works of Bach in the cathedral. Distler appeared as harpsichordist, assisted in a Bach program by Konzertmeister Kundrat, viol, and H. Kriegel, flute, in a concert played in St. Annenkloster.

Perhaps the most exciting events during this year were those connected with the restorations of both the St. Jakobi organs. This work had been in the planning stage for quite some time with Distler, his brother-in-law Erich Thienhaus, and the Lübeck organ builder Karl Kemper cooperating on the specifications for the restorations. A musical celebration on Sept. 6 marked the first voyage of the new ship *Tannenberg* with a Bach program. Distler was at the rear-gallery organ, but a notice on the printed program announced that only part of the organ would be playable because of the rebuilding still in progress.

A visit by the famous boys' choir of the Thomaskirche in Leipzig, conducted by Karl Straube, allowed Distler another opportunity to work with this famous organist and conductor. For the concert on Oct. 5 Distler assisted at the organ of St. Jakobi in the following program:

I. Froberger	Ricercare in E Minor
Philipp Denlich	*Gloria Patri*
Senfl	*Da Jakob nu das kleid ansah*
David Köler	Psalm III
Johann Eccard	*Uebers Gebirg Maria geht*
Gallus (Handl)	*Pater noster*
II. Pachelbel	Organ Chorale, *O Lamm Gottes unschuldig*
Schütz	Three Cantiones Sacrae for 4-part choir
	In dich, Herr, hab' ich gehofft
	Komm, ich bitte, in mein Herze
	Cantate Domino canticum novum
III. Bach	Fugue in E-flat
Bach	*Singet dem Herrn ein neues Lied*
	Motet for double chorus

Great success awaited Distler at the Kassel *Musiktage,* Oct. 9 through 13. This convention, attended by 800 foreign guests and many more Germans, culminated in two events on Sunday, Oct. 13. In the morning a chamber music concert was presented in the Aula der Malwida of the Mensenburgschule. This program included a gamba concerto and a concerto for three violins and orchestra by Telemann; a hitherto unknown oboe trio by Handel; the Bach cantata

Meine Seele rühmt und preist; and the Bach fifth Brandenburg Concerto, with Hugo Distler playing the brilliant harpsichord solo part.

The evening concert was presented by the Lübeck *Sing- und Spielkreis* in the Martinuskirche. Here Bruno Grusnick conducted a program consisting entirely of Distler's works. Opening with the D-minor Ricercare for organ, the program continued with a *missa brevis,* consisting of the "Kyrie" and "Gloria" from the *Deutsche Choralmesse,* opus 3. Two motets followed, *Ich wollt, dass ich daheime wär* and the *Totentanz,* both from the *Geistliche Chormusik,* opus 12. Then followed two world premieres, the motet based on *Wachet auf, ruft uns die Stimme* and the organ partita on the same chorale.

Newspapers all over Germany reported the tremendous impressions made by Distler's music at this concert. Typical of the press acclaim granted the young composer was this quotation from the magazine *Lied und Volk.* It was illustrated with the sketch of the composer, made during a rehearsal for the *Wachet auf* motet by an artist named Sprick.

> Hugo Distler is the great hope of German church music, or more succinctly, of German music. One had to carry this impression away from Kassel. Not only is he well educated, but, even more, he has greatness and depth of spirit. With great seriousness his church music penetrates the meaning of the words. Perhaps the best that one could say is this: the possibilities are placed in his hands; the maturity and completeness of his creations will depend less on the further increase of his means for expression and technical ability than on the degree of his inner maturing and the discipline with which he employs the gifts given him. For this the group with which he associates will, in all probability, be a help to him.[54]

On the way home from Kassel the Lübeckers presented the same program of Distler works in the St. Johanneskirche in Lüneburg on Oct. 14.

That October 1935 was quite a month for Hugo Distler cannot be disputed! Three festive days, Oct. 25, 26, and 27, were reserved for the inauguration and reconsecration of the newly rebuilt St. Jakobi organs.

The celebration, designed to consist mainly of works by J. S. Bach, began with a harpsichord recital in the St. Annenkloster by

Günther Ramin. This program included the sixth French Suite (E-major), the Goldberg Variations, and the Chromatic Fantasy and Fugue in D Minor. The Neupert harpsichord was loaned to the museum by Distler.

On the following day Ramin opened the 52-rank gallery organ with another all-Bach program:

I. Prelude and Fugue in C Major (Peters, II, 7)

II. Prelude and Fugue in A Major

III. Prelude and Fugue in B Minor

IV. Three Chorale Preludes
O Mensch, bewein dein Sünde gross
Nun freut euch, lieben Christen g'mein
Komm, Heiliger Geist (Leipzig, 18)

V. Passacaglia and Fugue in C Minor

The festival church service on Sunday morning was cited by Dr. Fred Hamel as an exemplary one:

> . . . A church service began, which in its strong Lutheran tradition moved the hearers deeply. The pastor intoned the liturgy, using the ancient Gregorian tones. In a living sense of unity, really without comparison, the responses were sung now by the choir in unison, now by the congregation accompanied by the organ.
>
> From this wonderful liturgy the polyphonic music also grew, a splendid blooming plant from fruitful earth. Following the commandment "Sing to the Lord a new song," it represented the spirit of the present in the midst of full awareness of the tradition of the past. The music consisted exclusively of works by the Jakobi organist Hugo Distler. Individual selections from these, the motet *Lobe den Herren,* the melismatic *Amen,* we had already learned to know as examples of a strong and independently growing creative talent. Never, however, had we experienced them as here, in their deep, spiritual, liturgical reason for being.
>
> Here the art of music found the highest consecration and impressiveness, when, after the *Kyrie eleison,* a solo voice was lifted in naive and jubilant expression of the liturgical words of the *Gloria,* while the choir accompanied this with the German *Allein Gott,* or when the organ referred back to the tune of the sermon hymn with a majestic toccata on *Wachet auf.*[55]

The final event in this festival weekend was the concert by the *Dresden Kreuzchor,* conducted by Rudolf Mauersberger, which took place at eight o'clock that evening (Oct. 27). Distler was again at the historic smaller organ for a program that was originally to have been an all-Bach one. A special notice inserted in the program announced, however, that, at the expressed wish of Mauersberger, the *Kreuzchor* would open the program with the 6-part *Deutsche Choralmesse,* opus 3, by Hugo Distler. The program which followed included these Bach works:

    I. Organ: Choralpartita *Sei gegrüsset, Jesu gütig*

   II. Choir: Motet V, *Komm, Jesu, komm*

 III. Organ: Toccata, Adagio, and Fugue in C Major

 IV. Choir: Motet II, *Der Geist hilft unsrer Schwachheit auf*

  V. Organ: Fantasy in G Major

Distler's organ playing was singled out for the highest praise by the *Musik und Kirche* critic, who called it the "highpoint of the evening." [56] The local critics also noted the remarkable growth in Distler's powers as an organist, commenting particularly on the "excitement and rhythmic vitality" of his playing.[57]

The regular musical program of St. Jakobi, revitalized by the rebuilding of these two distinguished organs, continued with the 30th Musical Vespers on Nov. 24. Distler played the larger organ in a repetition of the Kassel program that included the *Wachet auf* compositions.

Vespers 31, the last for 1935, featured a performance of Distler's *Weihnachtsgeschichte,* opus 10, on the second day of Christmas.

Distler was not so often heard at the Jakobi organs during 1936. His duties as a teacher in two conservatories (Lübeck and Berlin-Spandau), his ever progressing work of composition, and his guest appearances in many German cities may be cited as reasons for the number of guest organists to appear in the vesper series for 1936. In addition to musical reasons the religious climate in Germany during the year was decidedly unhealthful for all, and especially for members of the Lutheran churches.

To clarify the situation of the German church at this time, a brief survey of the Nazi years is necessary. Immediately after Hitler's appointment to the chancellorship in 1932 the more fanatical Nazis among the Lutherans formed a "German Christians' Faith Movement," led by Ludwig Mueller, army chaplain of the East Prussian district. This group supported the Nazi doctrines of racial purity and state leadership.

Opposing this group was a minority group called the "Confessional Church." These Lutherans, eventually led by Pastor Martin Niemöller, opposed the Nazi ideology, especially the racial doctrines and the philosophies of Rosenberg. There was, of course, much jockeying for power. In May 1934 a general synod at Barmen declared the "Confessional Church" to be the legitimate Protestant church in Germany, and this was confirmed by a special meeting in Niemöller's church in Dahlem, a suburb of Berlin, in November 1934. The Gestapo responded by arresting 700 "Confessional Church" pastors; an attempt at compromise was led by Dr. Zöllner, a man respected by all factions. The "Confessional Church" still, however, considered itself the legitimate national church, and stated these views in a memorandum to Hitler in May 1936. This memorandum further denounced the anti-Christian and anti-Semitic actions of the Nazis and demanded an end to state interference in church affairs. The result was that hundreds of pastors were arrested, the funds of the church confiscated, collections forbidden, and one of the signers of the memorandum, Dr. Weissler, murdered at Sachsenhausen concentration camp.[58]

Pastor Kühl was one of the leaders of the "Confessional Church," Grusnick, a member of the *Bruder-Rat,* the brothers' council.

For the 32d Musical Vespers at St. Jakobi the guest organist was Prof. Fritz Heitmann of Berlin, the choir, the Lübeck *Sing- und Spielkreis,* Grusnick conducting. The 33d Vespers found Distler again at the small organ, with the choir of the Hamburg *Volksmusikschule* conducted by Walter Kraft. Compositions by Distler (*Wie schön leuchtet der Morgenstern* and the G-minor Chaconne from Partita, opus 8/I, both for organ); Pepping (choral selections from the *Spandauer Chorbuch*); and Walter Kraft (7-part motet *Hallelujah! Singt und seid froh,* and 10-part chorale setting for two choirs, *Wie schön leuchtet*) were heard at this program.

Guest organist for Vespers 34 (March 8, 1936) was Domkantor Hans Heintze of Dresden.

In March Distler composed in a few short hours the burial motet *In der Welt habt ihr Angst* as a memorial to his mother-in-law, Frau Thienhaus, who had died during this month.[59]

Distler was organist for a program sung by the *Singkreis* at the Christuskirche in Altona-Othmarschen, near Hamburg, on March 22. Works of the Baroque masters were programed: Buxtehude, Pachelbel, Bach.

The 35th St. Jakobi Vespers on April 10 (Good Friday) presented the Schütz *St. Matthew Passion* and the G-minor Fantasy of Pachelbel, the Bach chorale prelude *O Haupt voll Blut und Wunden,* and the Bach C-minor Fantasy.

Two important engagements in Hamburg were outstanding events of 1936 for Hugo Distler. At a chamber orchestra concert on April 29 he played the premiere of his Concerto for Harpsichord and String Orchestra, opus 14. The Hamburg Chamber Orchestra was conducted by Dr. Hans Hoffmann, to whom the work is dedicated; the place was the Conventgarten, Grosser-Saal, in Fuhlentwiete; and the program also included J. S. Bach's Concerto in A Minor for Harpsichord, Flute, and Violin, the K. P. E. Bach Sinfonia in B-flat for Strings and Harpsichord, and *Musik Nr. II* for Chamber Orchestra of Flute and Strings, by Gerhard Maasz.

The second great success in Hamburg was centered on the *Kirchenmusiktage,* May 6 through 9. In the St. Jakobi Parish House (Hamburg) Distler spoke on "The Proclamation of the Word Through Contemporary Church Music" on Thursday afternoon, May 7; following this address he conducted a singing hour. On Friday, May 8, Grusnick led an hour of singing in the morning, spoke on "The Duties of the Church Musician" in the afternoon, and conducted an *Abendmusik* of Distler's compositions at the main church of St. Jakobi in the evening. This program was rather different in its conception.

I. *Entrance*
   Organ: Chaconne in G Minor (Partita, opus 8/I)
   Pastor: Introit and Prayer

II. *German Mass*
   Organ: Intonation for the *Kyrie* hymn
   Congregation: *Kyrie* hymn
   Choir: 8-part *Kyrie* and 4-part *Gloria* with a melismatic
      solo voice
   Congregation: *Gloria* hymn
   Organ: Ricercare on the *Credo* hymn
   Congregation: *Credo* hymn
   Choir: 6-part *Credo* (*Choralmesse,* op. 3)

Organ: Prelude to the *Agnus Dei* hymn
Congregation: *Agnus Dei* hymn
Choir: 6-part *Agnus Dei* with a melismatic solo voice (From the *Choralmesse,* op. 3)
Organ: Fugue in C Major

III. *The Easter Gospel*
Pastor: 1st Gospel: Matt. 28:1-15
Organ: Prelude to the motet
Choir: Chorale Motet, *Mit Freuden zart*
Pastor: 2d Gospel: Matt. 28:16 ff.
Choir: Motet, *Erstanden ist der Herre Christ*
Pastor: 3d Gospel: Luke 24:13-31
Choir, with Instruments:
   Chorale Cantata, *Christ, der du bist der helle Tag*
Congregation: Final stanza of the chorale, *Christ, der du bist der helle Tag*

IV. *Conclusion*
Pastor: Lord's Prayer and Benediction
Choir: *Amen*
Organ: Partita, *Christ, der du bist der helle Tag,* from opus 8/III

Distler was at the organ (and at his Neupert harpsichord for the cantata) for this program. Margarete Baum from Kassel was soprano soloist, and the choir was the Lübeck *Singkreis*. The program was very well received, a model for the integration of contemporary church music into the liturgy.

Just prior to the Hamburg church music gathering Distler had performed the harpsichord concerto in Lübeck (May 5) with the same orchestra with which he had played the first performance, the Hamburg chamber group under Dr. Hoffmann. Further performances of this work, with Distler playing the solo part, were heard later in this summer at the Composers' Festival in Weimar and at the *Musiktage* in Kassel.

Sandwiched between concert dates was an event of personal significance: the birth of a son, Andreas, on May 28, 1936. There was little time to spend at home, however, for the first week in June was devoted to a "Hugo Distler Choral Week" at the town of Ratzeburg, not far from Lübeck. Under the direction of Bruno Grusnick the participants were treated to a week of Distler's choral music. On two days Distler himself was there, and these days were reported to be the highpoints of the week, a thrill to those who were permitted to learn the music from the composer himself.[60]

On Saturday evening in the old cathedral founded by Henry the Lion, an *Abendmusik* was given as a festive ending to the week of learning and singing. All the choral music was by Distler. Early the next morning a motorboat took the participants to Lübeck, where they heard Walter Kraft play the *Totentanz* organ at St. Marien. That evening, before the altar of the St. Jakobikirche, the closing took place. Jan Bender, one of Distler's pupils at the Lübeck Conservatory and organist at St. Gertrud's church, played Distler's *Wachet auf* as a prelude. Then the group again sang a selection of Distler choral works. "Here it was apparent that the creations of Hugo Distler in the Jakobikirche with its organs, and the work of Bruno Grusnick with his *Singkreis,* made a wonderful unity in the service of the Most High," wrote Wilhelm Stever in *Musik und Kirche.*

Another workshop, *Protestant Church Music,* was sponsored by the *Arbeitskreis für Hausmusik,* Kassel, from July 25 through Aug. 15. In the final week Distler was there to conduct and lecture about his own music.

The well-earned vacation during that summer of 1936 was spent in the scenic region near Berchtesgaden in Bavaria. Distler's inventive mind did not rest during this time, however, for he was busily working on a libretto for an opera. The subject was Veit Stoss, a medieval artist, and the title of the work was *Die Schalksknechte Gottes.* (The Unfaithful Servants of God). The yellowing pages of the copybook in which the text was completed announce that it was to have been an opera in five acts, ten scenes. It was Distler's plan to bind the opera and oratorio closer together, to make the chorus more important. Unfortunately the work was never realized.

Back in Lübeck Walter Kraft featured three Distler compositions in his sixth *Abendmusik* at the St. Marienkirche on Sept. 9: *Wachet auf, es tut euch Not,* Little Partita for Organ *Christ, der du bist der helle Tag,* and the *Wachet auf* motet.

Grusnick took his *Sing- und Spielkreis* on a tour of central Germany from Oct. 4 through 18. Distler did not travel with the group, but his music was sung in many new places, for the tour included Lüneburg, Ebstorf (bei Uelzen), Braunschweig, Goslar, Kassel, Hildesheim, and Halberstadt. Distler's pupil Jan Bender was organist for the various programs.

The Kassel *Musiktage* were scheduled in 1936 for Oct. 9—11. Here Distler performed his harpsichord concerto. The 36th Saint Jakobi Vespers, Sunday, Nov. 1, featured the playing of both organs. The organ music, all Bach, included the 6-voice *Aus tiefer Not* from the *Klavierübung,* Part III; the Distler favorite Toccata, Adagio, and Fugue, and the Prelude and Fugue in E-flat, also from the *Klavierübung,* III.

Vespers 37, on the first Sunday in Advent, included Jan Bender's *Organ Toccata* (1936), Distler's *Nun freut euch,* the *Kleine Adventsmusik,* and, spread through the service, the organ partita *Nun komm, der Heiden Heiland.*

Vespers 38, on Dec. 27, once again presented the *Weihnachtsgeschichte,* opus 10. Organist for the service was Ika Bräck.

The winter of 1936—37 was a most troubled time in the war between the "Confessional Church" and the Nazi government. Pastor Kühl, the leader of this group in Lübeck, was placed under house arrest, forbidden to preach in the church, and eventually exiled from the territory.

On Feb. 12, 1937, Dr. Zoellner resigned from the church committee because he had been restrained from visiting Lübeck to see the nine pastors who had been arrested there.

At this same time, while Pastor Kühl was forbidden to set foot in Lübeck, Bruno Grusnick was forced to serve a short-term military obligation in Hamburg, so Distler was left without a close friend or confidant in the city. The situation appeared so hopeless to him that he began looking around for another position.

It was not difficult to find one; an offer came to him for a full-time position at the conservatory in Berlin-Spandau, to which he had been commuting during the past four years. Distler had already agreed to accept this position, when another offer came to him from the Hochschule in Stuttgart; always an impulsive person, Distler accepted this position although he had already given his word to the Spandau school. The advantage of Stuttgart, as Distler saw it, was the guarantee that he would have a good choir to direct.

The school at Spandau was, quite naturally, irate, since the administration there had passed over several other possible candidates to appoint Distler. Distler, hoping to get out of all the uproar, feigned sickness and refused to answer any telephone calls. Grusnick, by this time returned from Hamburg, was forced to deal with these calls himself, although the parties concerned kept insisting that it was Herr Distler to whom they wished to speak.

Somehow or other Distler managed to ignore the fact that he was committed to the Spandau position, and on April 1, 1937, he left Lübeck for Stuttgart. When Pastor Kühl eventually returned to St. Jakobi, the triumvirate was no more; Distler was already gone, succeeded by Johannes Brennecke, director of the Lübeck *Konservatorium*.[61]

The Stuttgart Years

Distler succeeded Professor Dr. Hugo Holle at the *Württembergische Hochschule für Musik* in Stuttgart; his position included the teaching of form and analysis, composition, and choral conducting, and he conducted two school choirs. At first his position in Stuttgart was complicated by the fact that the Nazi-oriented students boycotted his efforts because he was a "church musician." As his work became better known, some of this anti-Distler feeling disappeared, but his relationship to the student body in Stuttgart was never a completely free and easy one.

At first the Distlers lived in the city, at Birkenstrasse 15; later, however, they moved to the suburb of Vaihingen an der Filder, far from the noise of the city. Here, at Ammoneten Weg 5, in a community of good neighbors, many of whom were also artists — actors, painters, musicians — Distler passed his happiest years.

One of Distler's projects was the founding of the *Esslinger Singakademie,* an oratorio society. This he did shortly after his arrival in Stuttgart. Two of his neighbors, the painter Heinrich von Kralik and Dr. Walter Supper, an organist, introduced him to Hans Kienlin, whom Distler asked to be business manager of the group.

The singers necessary for such a venture were available, for a former oratorio society, now defunct, had numbered many singers, and Helmut Bornefeld, who had conducted a chamber choir in Esslingen, had recently gone to another position in Heidenheim;

56

these choir members were all available and happy to find another choral group.

The very first rehearsal of the group has been described by Frau Hellmut Typke. Distler was a few moments late coming into the rehearsal room, and the assembled singers, most of whom did not know him by sight, were full of anticipation wondering what their new conductor would be like. When, quite suddenly, he stood before them, a thin, pale, nervously energetic young man, somewhat "poor of body" as the local saying went, a general gasp of surprise could be heard. He looked "too young" to be a teacher at the Hochschule.

His rehearsal technique, however, soon left no doubt that he was well qualified to hold his teaching position! He promptly listened to each individual voice, then heard them in small groups of twos and threes, insisting in each case that solo voices subordinate themselves to the group, working, above all, for a pure blending of the voices.

The first performance of the *Esslinger Singakademie* was Carl Orff's new edition of Monteverdi's *Orfeo*. The performance, according to Frau Erika Kienlin, one of the singers, "seemed to break like an enlightenment over everyone; there was a charm, a delight which no one could take away from the singers."[62]

Distler was quite enchanted by Orff's work at this time; an event of 1937 in Frankfurt am Main was the first performance of Orff's novel *Carmina Burana* for chorus and orchestra, a work based on the medieval Latin poems of the Goliards, or wandering scholars, discovered in the old Bavarian Abbey of Benediktbeuern by Johann Schmeller, who published them under the name *Carmina Burana* in 1847. Ninety years later the music Orff wrote to some of these texts caused a sensation; Distler attended the premiere and was much impressed by the newness and rhythmic vitality of the work.

Another work Distler heard during this period was Hindemith's *Mathis der Maler;* always intrigued by the operas of others, Distler never finished one of his own, although various ideas for scenarios and libretti occupied him at intervals.

The summer months offered freedom from teaching duties, and since Distler did not play for church services in Stuttgart, his time was much freer for composition and for relaxation. He dearly loved mountain climbing, and being near the Bavarian Alps, he found it possible to indulge in this enjoyment.

Because he did not have a church organ at his disposal (how he must have longed for his beloved St. Jakobi!), it became obvious that Distler would need a practice instrument of some sort. He corresponded with the builders Kemper (Lübeck) and Steinmeyer (Oettingen), but finally decided to order an instrument from Paul Ott of Göttingen.

The disposition of the instrument was drawn up in consultation with Erich Thienhaus, his brother-in-law, who was an acoustician. The outward aspects of the disposition, that is, the case and the console, were designed by Helmut Bornefeld. The instrument was delivered early in 1938.

Another occupation Distler found relaxing was learning how to drive his first automobile; others did not find it quite so relaxing! Frau Distler related laughingly how her husband noticed one of his students riding in a bus, pulled the car up beside the bus, and blithely carried on a conversation with the student while both vehicles were in motion, not realizing that the roadway was getting progessively, and quickly, narrower. Disaster was avoided, but Distler was soon driving on the sidewalk! As the composer himself wrote ". . . learning to drive a car gives me, with my temperament, certain difficulties, but also much that is funny. . . ."

In early August Distler was again in north Germany conducting a *Singwoche,* according to an announcement in *Musik und Kirche* for 1937. He also composed a *Konzertstück* for piano and orchestra which was not published until after his death.

The most noted and best-attended of the many various church music festivals to be held in Germany during the decade of the 30s was that which took place in Berlin from Oct. 7 through 13, 1937, under the name *Das Fest der deutschen Kirchenmusik.* Approximately 20,000 visitors, many from other countries, attended this week-long demonstration of the incredible vitality that had erupted in the music of the Lutheran denominations between the two great wars.

Distler was well represented at this festival: On Friday, Oct. 8, there was organ music played by Professor Fritz Heitmann in the Eosanderkapelle; the compositions were by Johann Nepomuk David,

Eberhard Wenzel, and Distler. That same evening Heitmann directed a choral vesper in the cathedral, and Distler was again represented on the program.

The president of the *Reichsmusikkammer,* Dr. Peter Raabe, conducted the Berlin Philharmonic in a concert of works by David, Fortner, Pepping, Zillinger, and Distler at noon on Sunday, Oct. 10. Walter Kraft was soloist in the Distler harpsichord concerto at this program.

At the nine o'clock Matins the following day, works by Distler shared a program with compositions by Carl Gerhardt and Gottfried Müller, and on Oct. 12 an eight-o'clock concert in the Gustav Adolf-Kirche was composed entirely of Distler's compositions. The Grünewald church choir was under the direction of Professor Wolfgang Reimann, and Walter Kraft was at the organ for a program that included the *Weihnachtsgeschichte,* opus 10, two double-choir settings of the *Kyrie* and *Gloria,* the motet *Ich wollt, dass ich daheime wär,* and both organ partitas.

The Nazi press was rather disconcerted by the tremendous success of this gathering. According to a decree of Dr. Goebbels, the propaganda minister, critics in all fields of art were not allowed to praise or to blame, but merely to describe (Nov. 27, 1936),[63] but the Nazi press promptly branded much of the new church music as "un-German," and "degenerate," a category that was applied to Distler's harpsichord concerto in particular. In fact, it was only through the intervention of a nameless, church-minded employee of the propaganda ministry that any reports of the conference got into the newspapers at all. An order had been issued that the festival was to be blanketed by editorial silence, but the order was never transmitted.[64]

But reactions from other sources did not follow the official pronouncements: Cathedral organist Josef Hedar from Lund, Sweden, wrote:

> This festival has shown in an overwhelming way that evangelical church music today in Germany is possessed with the same mighty power that it had in the days of Schütz, Buxtehude, and Bach. It has also shown with all clearness where we will have to look for examples and guideposts for the renewal of our Swedish church music.[65]

In the following month Distler visited Lübeck. At the invitation of the St. Jakobi council he once more officiated at the organ for a vesper service of his own works. Pastor Kühl was back in Lübeck, the resistance of the "Confessional Church" having been successfully broken by the Nazis. Pastor Niemöeller, who had been the leader of this truly heroic group, had been arrested on July 1, and was currently confined in the Moabit prison in Berlin. During the terrible months of persecution throughout 1937 more than 807 pastors and leading laymen of the "Confessional Church" had been arrested, and many of them were incarcerated in concentration camps.[66]

It was both fitting and tragic that the Vespers on that *Totensonntag* 1937 (Nov. 21) should include the chorale *Ach wie flüchtig, ach wie nichtig,* prefaced by Distler's chorale prelude, and the *Totentanz* motet. Distler played his partita on *Jesus Christus, unser Heiland,* the *Wachet auf* partita, and the Ricercare in D Minor.

On Dec. 21, 1937, the *Reichsmusikkammer* established a music examining board to "protect the German people against the influence of undesirable and deleterious music, such as phonograph records by Jews and Negroes, or non-Aryan printed music." [67] Examiners were appointed in various regions as well; their duty was to visit all private music teachers and to determine whether they were teaching in a manner favorable to the Nazi party. Following a restful Christmas vacation in Allgäu, Distler was appointed one of the examiners for the Stuttgart area, a task which distressed him greatly, but one which he took on, hoping in a small way to help those whom he was forced to examine. Many teachers were declared undesirable and thereby lost their only means of livelihood; Distler hoped by accepting membership in the board to offer leniency to a few of these unfortunates.

The peacefulness of the quiet home in Vaihingen rather than the ugliness of the political world was reflected in the compositions occupying Distler during these months. To texts of his friend, the poet Heinz Grunow, Distler wrote various a cappella secular songs, which were published as his *Neues Chorliederbuch.* Eight sections comprise this work; the titles alone hint at the contents: (1) Peasant Songs; (2 and 3) Love Songs; (4—7) Calendar Sayings, one for each month of the year; (8) Happy Songs, three songs to texts not by Grunow.

Some of these latest compositions were heard on the second program of the *Esslinger Singakademie.* Again to quote Frau Kienlin,

"Distler had composed these songs with such lightness and yet with such a new kind of flowing rhythm! I remember most of all the compositions 'Ich brach drei dürre Reiselein' and 'Im Maien' from the *Kalendersprüche,* where suddenly the whole hall seemed to be dancing along with the music." [68]

The third undertaking of the *Singakademie* was the Bach *St. John Passion.* The performance took place in the Esslingen village church, the same edifice which shortly before had housed Dr. Peter Raabe of the *Reichsmusikkammer* in a performance of the same work. Distler decided to use only a small orchestral group to accompany the work, quite the opposite of the Raabe performance.

The rehearsals for this work remained in the memories of those who participated. Both Frau Kienlin and Frau Typke spoke of them in their "Erinnerungen." Humor had its part, to be sure: "Laugh," Distler would shout, "don't keep your heads buried in the scores — your expressions need to be alive!" or, "Don't sing 'queck,' but 'Weg, weg'!" A certain Frau Kauffmann noted a few of Distler's explanatory phrases in her score. To Chorus No. 40, *Durch dein Gefängnis,* he said "Simple and great." To No. 50, *Schreibe nicht,* "Irony!" No. 60, *Ruht wohl,* "Very great, but quietly." To *Das Grab, so euch bestimmet ist,* "Transfigured." [69]

Frau Typke wrote, "What these rehearsals and the performance cost him in spiritual involvement cannot be described and remains unforgettable. It was as if he had to endure the pains and death of the Savior himself, so completely was he overpowered by the recreation of this work." [70]

The *Johannespassion* was the final experience for the *Singakademie.* The Party no longer looked with favor on church music, and the group had to be disbanded. Distler's parting words to his friends and fellow workers were tinged with sadness, "It will have to be enough good fortune for you that you were able to sing *this* work."

Pastor Niemöller, brought to trial on March 2, 1938, before one of the "Special Courts" set up by the Nazi government to try crimes against the state, was acquitted of the main charge against him (underhand attacks against the government) but fined two thousand marks and sentenced to seven months' imprisonment; he was technically released since he had already served more than this amount of time, but as he left the courtroom he was retaken by the Gestapo and thereafter confined in concentration camps, first at Sachsenhausen and then at Dachau, until released by Allied troops at the end of the war.[71]

Other Protestant clergymen were forced to swear an oath of allegiance to Hitler or face the same fate as Niemöller; the vast majority thus bound itself legally and morally to uphold the Nazi doctrines, though these were contrary to Christian teaching.

On April 20, Distler wrote to Dr. Oskar Söhngen:

> Perhaps I would not have overcome this crisis if I had not had my family to fall back on, this completely private, last, and most secure circle, which, especially today, one must have or appropriate, if he is to have, anywhere, a possibility for continued existence.[72]

From the 18th to the 25th of April Distler was conducting an Easter *Singwoche* in the spa town of Bad Boll near Göppingen.

The first performance of the complete *Kalendersprüche* from the *Neues Chorliederbuch,* opus 16, was sung on April 28, 1938, by the *Oberhausener Singgemeinde* in the Aula of the Rhenish Friedrich Wilhelm University in Bonn. Karl-Heinrich Schweinsberg was organist for this program; Distler's friend Heinz Grunow, the young Berlin poet, whose words had been used for the texts of the "Calendar Sayings," wrote further recitations to introduce those choral settings not introduced by organ preludes. The program was arranged as follows: [73]

Organ: Toccata from Partita *Wachet auf,* op. 8/II
Organ: Prelude and chorale, *Das alte Jahr vergangen ist*
Choir: Kalenderspruch I (Peasant Rules)
Recitation
Choir: Kalenderspruch II (Candlemas)
Recitation
Choir: Kalenderspruch III (Beginning of Spring)
Organ: Prelude and chorale, *Mit Freuden zart*
Choir: Kalenderspruch IV (Eastertime)
Recitation
Choir: Kalenderspruch V (May)
Recitation
Choir: Kalenderspruch VI (Change of Season)
Recitation
Choir: Kalenderspruch VII (High Time)

Recitation
Choir: Kalenderspruch VIII (Harvest)
Recitation
Choir: Kalenderspruch IX (A Little Song of Thanksgiving)
Recitation
Choir: Kalenderspruch X (A Larger Song of Thanksgiving)
Organ: Bicinium, from Opus 8/III
Choir: Kalenderspruch XI (St. Martin's Day)
Organ: Chaconne from Partita *Nun komm, der Heiden Heiland,*
      op. 8/I
Choir: Kalenderspruch XII (The End of the Year)
Organ: Prelude and chorale, *Wie schön leuchtet der Morgenstern*

The results of the inspiration drawn from his new house organ were heard for the first time at the second Freiburg *Orgeltagung,* when selections from Distler's *Dreissig Spielstücke für Positiv* were played by Ernst Köhler. This conference placed emphasis on the reviving interest in small house organs and positives; also heard was another new Distler composition, the "sacred concerto" for soprano and organ, *Freuet euch in dem Herrn allerwege.*[74]

These simple but charming *Spielstücke,* together with the *Shorter Chorale Preludes* (opus 8/III), which had recently been published by Bärenreiter, were greeted with journalistic and critical acclaim.

From July 24 to 31 Distler headed a course for choral conductors in Bad Boll, under the auspices of the Association of Evangelical Church Choirs in Württemberg and the *Arbeitskreis für Hausmusik.*

Immediately following this engagement he traveled by car with Herr and Frau Hellmut Typke to Ratzeburg, where he led a *Singwoche* in which his two friends also took part. On Wednesday evening, Aug. 10, members of the Ratzeburg group sang in a Musical Vespers at St. Jakobi in Lübeck under Distler's direction, and Distler also played the small organ. Opening with Vincent Lübeck's Prelude and Fugue in E Major, the service continued with Distler's motet *Es ist das Heil uns kommen her,* his Ricercare for organ, Schütz's *Verleih uns Frieden gnädiglich,* the organ Fugue in E-flat of Bach, and closed with Distler's evening hymn *Die Sonne sinkt von hinnen.*

As early as January 27 of this year (1938), Distler had written to Oskar Söhngen, "The harpsichord concerto, too, is but a step on the way; I do not stand still; restlessness is in my blood, and I always want to be somewhere else. . . . Today I'll let myself be propelled where my 'Demon' wills it." [75]

In February 1938 an invitation to compose music for a film came from the Berlin producer Jürgen Fehling. The scenario, set in the Paris of 1857, the "Offenbach era" as Distler expressed it, interested the young composer; he wrote on Feb. 18 to Grabner for advice. Should he accept this commission?

Grabner responded by return mail that it would pain him immensely should Distler become entangled with the complexities of the film industry. The original overture was not followed by a contract, so the project fell through — to Grabner's relief, and, one gathers, to the relief of Distler as well.

During 1938 Distler's "Demon" drove him to composition at a frantic speed; by the spring of 1939 he had completed a monumental opus: The *Mörike-Chorliederbuch,* 48 settings of 40 poems from the Swabian pastor, so admired and ennobled by Hugo Wolf. Distler's settings, by employing a cappella choral forces throughout, are entirely different from those by the earlier Liedermaster; they offer Mörike's poems to an entirely different group of performers as well. Of the 48, 24 are for mixed chorus, 12 for women's voices alone, and 12 for men's voices.

The special place reserved for these works in the Distler catalog is suggested by the words of Bruno Grusnick, "The warmer sun and lovely landscape of Swabia allowed [Distler] to bring forth, as his loveliest offering, the *Mörike-Chorliederbuch.*" [76]

With these compositions, too, Distler achieved his supreme eminence as a choral conductor at the Festival of German Choral Music in Graz, Austria, in June 1939. Distler had been hoping through the spring to be able to take his Stuttgart Hochschule choir to this festival in Graz, but naturally such a trip required financial backing, which was very difficult to obtain from the ministry of education. As the time to make a final decision one way or the other approached, the answer seemed to change almost daily. At the last possible moment, the permission to take the choir was granted, and on his birthday, June 24, Distler and his group left Stuttgart by train for Graz.

As a birthday gift the choir presented him with a large basket of fresh fruit, a surprise, for in his agitation over all necessary arrangements, Distler had practically forgotten it *was* his birthday. Dark clouds and rain had been much in evidence in Stuttgart, but as soon as the touring group was well away from the city, the sun burst through the clouds, an omen, as it were, that better things were ahead. At least, this is how the group interpreted it, and, in these last days of peace, it was a valid interpretation, if only for a short time.[77]

Distler shared success in Graz with his old friend Bruno Grusnick, whose *Sing- und Spielkreis* was also in attendance. Never had Distler received such glowing reviews, never such high acclaim, universally bestowed. Not only his compositional talents received highest honor, but his exceptional abilities as a choral conductor as well.

Typical of the press reports was this excerpt from an article by Hans Weitzer in the *Südostdeutsche Tageszeitung:*

Hugo Distler, the German Composer, as Pathfinder

"Whenever the Gordian knot is ready, God sends an Alexander," a German poet said somewhere, sometime. . . . Hugo Distler, a true Alexander of choral music, cuts through Gordian knots. He pulls down the prison walls of barlines by breaking through them with the rhythmically daring flood of his ideas. Certainly barlines are there in the score. In reality, however, their effect is overcome, and they remain purely as helps to the notation.

Among all the choral composers heard thus far, we can say with assurance, Distler has won the most exuberant applause. The applause experienced the joy of virtually discovering itself, and it was propelled aloft from the springboard of the realization that once again German art was producing young masters.[78]

Such general acclaim and recognition was the climax to Distler's national recognition. Several magazine articles, beginning as early as 1933, had brought him into national prominence: in 1933 he had written a long article entitled *The Organ of Our Time;* in 1935 came the *Credo* for the young church music, *Concerning the Spirit of the New Church Music;* and in 1937 he had published an article concerning organ registration in Bach in the church music journal, *Musik und Kirche.* But these were all articles of interest to specialists, to fellow musicians; now came popular success and fame as well.

It was the Graz acclaim also that won for Distler his appointment to the Berlin-Charlottenburg *Hochschule für Musik,* for Professor Dr. Stein of this prestigious school heard Distler's music and saw his conducting at this German choral music festival, and it was he who tendered the invitation that took Distler from Stuttgart to Berlin.

Shortly before the Graz journey, in April 1939, Distler wrote the preface to his final organ work, a Trio Sonata in E Minor, and sent it off to his publishers. This work again shows the influence of his gem-like Ott house organ; its trio (3-voice) structure is organ music of the utmost purity; in conception it is chamber music, virtuose in its demands on the player.

Distler's only string quartet, opus 20/ II, in A Minor, also dates from this late Stuttgart period. The work reveals the composer's cognizance of Mozart and Beethoven, while the subject for the final movement is reminiscent of a Pachelbel organ fugue.

The summer of 1939 was idyllic. After Graz further duties, actually in the nature of pleasant excursions, included the annual *Singwochen* in Bad Boll and Ratzeburg, where the summer vacation was also spent. It was well to grasp happiness, for that summer was the last moment of even partial sanity in Europe. On Sept. 1, 1939, Hitler invaded Poland; France and Britain, honoring their alliance with that nation, declared war Sept. 3. The holocaust began.

During the early months of 1940 the first of Distler's encounters with the military draft occurred. He was summoned for a physical examination, and a letter to Oskar Söhngen in March contained the plea, "Have you any good counsel?" In April came a further note, "If you were to help me in the possibility I mentioned, I should be so thankful to you that I simply can't express it; this matter torments me endlessly. Require from me in return any service that I can perform for you." [79]

The actual move to Berlin, which occurred in late September 1940, was in large part to gain more security against war preparations and, hopefully, to be in an important enough position to be released from military obligation. This obsession with avoiding a soldier's uniform did not stem from any physical cowardice, although Distler was hardly of the most likely physical dimensions for armed service! Söhngen expressed one reason for Distler's agony in the face of this new war when he said, "He [Distler] had lost his only brother before Leningrad [presumably in the first war]; he himself did not wish, under any circumstances, to take part in a war which he held to be wrong." [80]

66

The final months in Stuttgart were utilized by Distler for the preparation of his harmony textbook, *Funktionelle Harmonielehre,* which was published in 1941 by Bärenreiter. Growing from his experiences teaching in Spandau, Lübeck, and Stuttgart, the book also owed a great deal in its approach to Grabner's textbook on linear counterpoint.

It was with real sadness that the Distlers left their country home in Vaihingen, their friendly neighbors, and the friends of the Stuttgart years. Distler wrote on Sept. 15, "As a matter of fact, I am passing these last weeks here in a certain quiet and idle melancholy in expectation of a greater and more difficult field of work to come." [81]

To complicate matters, Frau Distler was pregnant; but high honor and the course of fate could not be gainsaid. On Oct. 1, 1940, Hugo Distler began his work in Berlin.

Professor in Berlin

Distler's appointment in Berlin carried a very high honor with it for one who was only 32 years of age: the designation "Professor," which in German education is granted by the state ministry. His duties consisted of teaching choral conducting, theory, composition, and organ; he succeeded Professor Kurt Thomas, who moved on to become director of the new musical *Gymnasium* in Frankfurt.[82]

During this first fall in Berlin Distler took the chamber choir, founded by Thomas, for a small concert tour. In addition to this special group, Distler had another choral ensemble at the *Hochschule.* He was also busy with composition: incidental music to Tieck's drama *Ritter Blaubart* and the large secular cantata *Das Lied am Herde.* On Jan. 16, 1941, the Distlers' third child was born: a daughter, who was christened Brigitte. On this same day Distler received another summons from the *Wehrmacht,* a summons that was rescinded, but one which again caused much worry and nervous strain.

April 1, 1941, saw a further increase in his already formidable responsibilities. Distler was named conductor of the Berlin *Staats und Dom-Chor,* one of the highest honors that a choral conductor in Germany could attain. This venerable and artistically excellent group dated from 1842, when the king of Prussia called it into existence, and conferred on Felix Mendelssohn the title of General Music

Director. Distler succeeded Alfred Sittard in this position; Sittard, who had died at the age of 64, had filled this position on a full-time basis. For Distler it was the third choir in addition to all the teaching responsibilities he carried at the *Hochschule!*

Another complication concerned the lodging the Distler family had chosen. It was located at Kaiserstrasse 53 in Strausberg bei Berlin, about 30 kilometers from the center of the city and an hour's drive from the *Hochschule.* As the war progressed, however, it seemed ever more wise to remain as far removed as possible from the strategic and bombing-prone inner city.

A concert report from Berlin in April 1941 had this to say,

> In a concert of the *Kantorei* of the *Staatliche Akademie für Musik,* Hugo Distler, the new conductor of the *Kantorei,* showed his many-sided talents as composer and conductor. Choruses from the *Mörike Liederbuch,* based on the old Baroque style with rhythmical and compositional refinements, showed him to be a figure of exceptional individuality. His three-movement *Konzertstück für zwei Klaviere,* played with good taste and secure technique by Ursula Ebbecke and Brigitte Pfeiffer, showed a spirited use of new values.[83]

The series *Stunde der Kirchenmusik,* sponsored by the *Reichsverband für evangelische Kirchenmusik,* also continued in this second winter of the war, with a series of contemporary compositions, in which Distler was represented, both as composer and as performer.

Vacation for the summer of 1941 was spent on the Baltic Sea at Albeck. Frau Distler and the children remained in this summer house on the Baltic from July through December to escape further the threats of bombings in the vicinity of Berlin. Distler was able to see them only on special weekends; the only good in this arrangement was that there was hardly any bombing in the east, and he could be somewhat reassured as to his family's safety. The further daily anxieties of caring for clothing and food added to his already insane schedule of work.

The *Hochschule Kantorei* made another concert tour in the fall of 1941, visiting Essen, Kassel, Bielefeld, Osnabrück, and other cities of northern and central Germany. Everywhere they were greeted with universal acclaim for the fineness of tone and diction and for the exceptional impressions made by the compositions of their conductor.

A long-standing fight with the party erupted in full force during this fall and made Distler's work at the cathedral very difficult. The Hitler-Jugend, the Nazi youth organization, was bitterly against church music, and it was able to sabotage the *Domchor* by scheduling organizational meetings involving the boys of the choir during Distler's rehearsal times. No matter when he scheduled rehearsals, the H-J would take all or part of his treble singers away. Finally Distler went directly to the ministry of education to see what could be done about it and received the blunt answer that he could expect this harrassment to continue; the only answer was for him to do "secular music with the boys, or continue his sacred music without them."

To fill the constantly diminishing ranks of singers in all parts of the *Domchor,* Distler was reduced to employing old professional singers, the "greybeards," as all the younger men were gradually being recruited for military service. These older men did not respond to direction, especially from one as young and particular as Distler, and this added to the tension and difficulty of his position.

Already during the Stuttgart years the plan for a great oratorio based on Greek mythology had occupied Distler's mind. During these work-filled Berlin years one of his major agonies was the lack of sufficient time for creative work. And yet, somehow through these tortured months of war and overwork, beginning in August 1941, he had managed to work on the text for this work, which he entitled *Die Weltalter* (The Ages of the World). The completed text, in typescript, is dated in Distler's handwriting Feb. 9, 1942. The work, which was to have been the musical realization of his old dream of a closer tie between opera and oratorio through a greater role for the chorus, was planned in three main sections: (1) *Arcadian Landscape* in four scenes, showing the seasons of the year; (2) *The Sons of Prometheus,* in which man, the self-elevating creative genius, would be extolled; and (3) the *Homecoming of the Palladians,* in which man, considering himself equal with the gods, is nearly destroyed, but saves himself through the realization of his own insufficiency by calling on the gods to save him. The finale was based on Sophocles' *Antigone,* "Much there is that is powerful, but none more powerful than man."

Although the text of this project was completed, only a few sketches for the music were ever made; nothing was completed in the musical score. The idea of composing a *St. John Passion* had also interested Distler for some time; of this projected composition a few sections were completed: already in September 1937 a single chorus, "Ah, Lord, I am not worthy," which was published separately; two choruses, which perhaps would have framed the complete work, were published as numbers eight and nine of the *Geistliche Chormusik,* opus 12: *Das ist je gewisslich wahr* (1 Tim. 1:15-16), which ended with the chorale *Ehre sei dir, Christe,* and *Fürwahr, er trug unsere Krankheit* (Is. 53:4-5), ending with the chorale *Ein Lämmlein geht und trägt die Schuld.* Besides these published bits, two *turba* choruses were left in manuscript: *Jesum von Nazareth* and *Wäre dieser nicht ein Uebeltäter,* as yet unpublished.[84]

About this time a prophetic and, in the light of the approaching end of Distler's suffering, a tragic letter was written to an old friend from the Lübeck days, Else Maiwald, organist of the Aegidienkirche in the north German city:

> How good that each of us has one comfort, which many men must do without at present: the certainty of an invisible kingdom, which, thank God, is not of this world. I feel more and more that Christ did not first of all mean a life after death when he spoke of this kingdom, but rather a life in which we find comfort at all times. Oh, that He would make us strong in this faith before all the horrors which perhaps still await us! [85]

The summer of 1942 offered a few days of vacation again at Albeck on the Baltic; at least it was a precious bit of time that Distler could spend with his wife and three children.

Back in the city, continuing the oppressing workload with which he was burdened, Distler began rehearsals for a performance of Heinrich Schütz's *Musikalische Exequien,* the first German Requiem, which he planned to perform with the *Staats- und Domchor* in November.

About Oct. 15 Distler apparently received another call to report for military service with the Panzer Division. In a letter to his wife, staying with the children at the summerhouse on the sea, Distler wrote, "You know how an indescribable loneliness remains, overpowering me, a feeling of being separated from everything and everybody." [86]

The feeling of hopelessness and the overwhelming load he had to bear broke Distler's spirit completely; the frustration of having no time to compose worked on his nervous spirit, and the likelihood that he would be forced to serve in Hitler's army finally drove him to a complete breakdown.

On the evening of Oct. 31 he went for a long walk, came home and played his beloved house organ for the last time, selecting the Bach A Major trio on *Allein Gott in der Höh' sei Ehr* from the Leipzig *Great Eighteen* chorale preludes as his farewell.

The following day, Nov. 1, was All Saints' Day. The tormented young man ended the living horror of his life. He moved a bed into the kitchen, placed a photograph of his dear family so he could see it, took a Bible in one hand and a brass cross in the other, turned on the gas, and lay down to sleep forever.

His farewell letter to his wife was almost childlike in its simplicity, "I have yet only one plea in the world: that *you* not be angry with me. Who knows more than you what a 'Lebensangst' has been with me all my life? All that I created remained beneath this sign." [87]

At the funeral service Hofprediger Dr. Döhring preached on the text: "For we are not contending against flesh and blood, but against the principalities, against the powers, against the world rulers of this present darkness, against the spiritual hosts of wickedness in the heavenly places" (Eph. 6:12). An uncounted number of friends gathered to say farewell to that part of Hugo Distler which was earthly. The wooden cross that marks his resting place in the *Waldfriedhof* in Stahnsdorf bei Berlin bears the text from St. John 16:33, which is also the text for one of his most beautiful motets, "In the world you have tribulation; but be of good cheer, I have overcome the world."

A few days after Distler's death came the news that he had been placed on the *Führerliste,* that enumeration of men who were important to the Third Reich on the homefront and who were thus exempted from military conscription: an ironic twist of fate that such a reassurance came only hours too late! Professor Dr. Hans Hoffman of Bielefeld took over the *Staats- und Domchor* for the scheduled Schütz Requiem, which was sung as a memorial to the late conductor.

In a sense Distler had written his own Requiem with his *Weltalter* text, just as Mozart did with his unpublished Requiem or Alban Berg with the Violin Concerto (to the memory of an angel). The words

that Distler had written were a personal prayer as well as a collective
one for the tragedy-bound German nation:

God!
Creator of all things!
From earth hast Thou created us
And to earth we return again at the end:
Dust to dust.

Only the spirit
Remains restless
And above space and time:
The spirit,
Which, triumphing over death and hell,
Springs from confinement
To touch Thy mystery,
Almighty God;
The spirit
In which Thou, in Thine own image, hast created us.[88]

What caused Hugo Distler to commit suicide? There is no simple
answer to explain the collapse of a sensitive, artistic mind. Contrib-
uting reasons already mentioned, included overwork, anxiety over
being forced to serve in Hitler's army, frustration resulting from a lack
of sufficient time for creative activity, the Nazi party's war against
the church, and the general disability of an artistic spirit to fit into
a totalitarian state.

In his book *Art Under a Dictatorship,* Helmut Lehmann-Haupt
expressed the functions of art to a dictator:

. . . The language of art speaks most eloquently to the individual. In order to survive, the totalitarian state must draw the
individual away from himself, absorb him into a communal scheme
of life that tolerates growth and development of the personality
only along narrowly prescribed lines. Art that is the expression
of individual search, of experiment, of intuitive play, art that
penetrates the surface of the visual worlds, that is prophetic,
sensitive, apprehensive, art that challenges the individual, that
demands concentration, effort, art that heightens perception, sharp-
ens the eye, nourishes thought — that art cannot be tolerated by
the dictator. He must eliminate it. . . . He must demand art that
creates the illusion of a secure, serene world, that hides the sinister
motives and the terror.[89]

And Christine Bourbeck has said: *Dichter sind Menschen der
feinsten Antennen, sie erleben am tiefsten, was eine Zeit bewegt und*

wovon sie sich umtreiben lässt. ("Poets are men of the finest sensitivity, who experience most deeply the currents of the time and what underlying movements are causing them.")

Distler's lifelong preoccupation with the eschatological, with death and with what comes after life (as expressed by the prominence of such texts in his sacred music) led him naturally and finally to the only solution that seemed to him practical and honorable. "That his heart broke showed the depth of that heart," wrote an unknown poet at Distler's death; "he saw things the rest of us were too weak and pale to admit." [90]

NOTES TO CHAPTER 1

1. Osbert Sitwell, *Those Were the Days: Panorama with Figures* (London, 1938), pp. 194–197.
2. Gurlitt edited the contemporary facsimile edition of this work, published by Bärenreiter, Kassel, in 1958. (*Documenta Musicologica,* Series I, No. XIV)
3. See Christhard Mahrenholz, "Fünfzehn Jahre Orgelbewegung," *Musik und Kirche,* X (1938), 8-28.
4. Norman Demuth, *Musical Trends in the Twentieth Century* (London, 1952), p. 188.
5. Karl Straube, preface to *Alte Meister des Orgelspiels* (Leipzig, 1926).
6. This information is based on the author's conversation with KMD Bruno Grusnick, St. Jakobikirche in Lübeck, July 3, 1962. In a letter to Hermann Grabner (Jan. 18, 1937), Distler remarked that he would be "returning to his native environment," because his father had been from Stuttgart. (Grusnick, "Hugo Distler und Hermann Grabner." *Musica,* XVIII [1964], 61.)
7. Information based on the author's conversation with the composer's widow, Frau Waltraut Distler, Marquartstein/Obb., July 29, 1962.
8. Letter from Distler to the St. Jakobi Church Council, Nov. 7, 1930; quoted in Bruno Grusnick, "Wie Hugo Distler Jakobiorganist wurde," *Musik und Kirche,* XXVIII (1958), 100.
9. Günther Ramin: born Oct. 15, 1898, in Karlsruhe; died Feb. 27, 1956, in Leipzig. In 1918 he became organist of the Thomaskirche in Leipzig, in 1920 professor of organ at the Leipzig Conservatory, and in 1939 he was successor to Karl Straube as Thomaskantor.
10. Hermann Grabner: born May 12, 1886, in Graz; studied with Max Reger in Leipzig in 1910. Professor of composition, Leipzig Cons. in 1924.
11. C. A. Martienssen: born Dec. 6, 1881, in Güstrow; died March 1, 1955, in Berlin. Professor of piano, Leipzig Conservatory, 1914–1934.
12. Hermann Grabner, "Erinnerungen an Hugo Distler," unpublished memoir; text given to the author through the courtesy of Frau Waltraut Distler.
13. Gerhard Kappner, "In Memoriam Hugo Distler," *Musik und Gottesdienst,* XII (1958), 78.
14. Grusnick, "Wie Hugo Distler . . . ," p. 100.
15. Ibid.
16. Ibid.

17. Siegfried Dähling, born Aug. 18, 1901, in Lübeck; 1925, choirmaster at St. Aegidien; 1930, organist at the Reformed Church, both in Lübeck.

18. Hilde Schneider, another native Lübecker; 1936–39, choirmaster at Saint Aegidien.

19. Martin Toppius, a Leipziger. Thus the selection was to be made from two local musicians and two nonlocal ones.

20. Bruno Grusnick, born Oct. 18, 1900, in Spandau. Choirmaster at Sankt Jakobikirche, Lübeck, since Easter, 1930.

21. Professor Wilhelm Stahl, lifelong Lübeck musician, organist of the Matthäikirche and later of the cathedral; author of the second volume of Lübeck's Musical History, published in 1952 by Bärenreiter, Kassel.

22. Grusnick, "Wie H. Distler," p. 103.

23. Ibid., p. 101.

24. Ibid., p. 102.

25. The Sonata for Two Pianos appeared in 1931 as Distler's opus one. The chorale motet *Herzlich lieb hab' ich dich, o Herr,* for 8-part double choir, was published in 1931 as opus 2 (Breitkopf and Härtel, *Partitur-Bibliothek,* No. 3348). The Trio mentioned by the composer was never published.

26. Grusnick, "Wie H. Distler," p. 104.

27. Ibid.

28. Ibid., pp. 105 f.

29. Axel Werner Kühl, "Vesper in St. Jakobi," *Lübeckische Blätter,* 73 (1931), 86; quoted in Ursula von Rauchhaupt, *Die vokale Kirchenmusik Hugo Distlers* (Gütersloh: Gütersloher Verlagshaus Gerd Mohn, 1963).

30. The program of this vesper, and all subsequent vespers, are collected in Pastor Axel Werner Kühl's scrapbook, preserved in the *Distler-Archiv,* Lübeck. For a complete list of the vesper programs, see Appendix A.

31. Ursula von Rauchhaupt, *Die vokale Kirchenmusik Hugo Distlers,* p. 10.

32. The author asked KMD Bruno Grusnick about this work in a conversation on August 25, 1962. Some parts are still extant, but a complete score is no longer available. It was never published. Distler mentioned his work for this cantata, without great enthusiasm, in his letter to Hermann Grabner (April 17, 1931). "It was," he wrote, "necessary for financial reasons," but it interrupted his preferred work on a harpsichord concerto. (Grusnick, "Hugo Distler und Hermann Grabner," 57).

33. Leopold Thieme, "Abendmusik in St. Katherinen," *Lübeckische Blätter,* 73 (1931), 438.

34. It was the author's privilege in July 1962 to see the presentation copy of this work with hand-drawn illustrations which the composer presented to his fiancée, Waltraut Thienhaus, as a Christmas gift. The information concerning the premiere performance is from Frau Distler.

35. Waldemar Klink, choral conductor in Nuremberg.

36. Kurt Klein, "In Memoriam Hugo Distler," *Musica,* VI (1952), 452.

37. J. Hennings, "Lübeckisches Kammerorchester," *Lübeckische Blätter,* 74 (1932), 287.

38. See Rudolf Maack, in *Musik und Kirche,* IV (1932), 246.

39. J. Hennings, *Lübeckische Blätter,* 74 (1932), 638.

40. This and all following facts about the deterioration of German musical life is taken from Nicholas Slonimsky's *Music Since 1900* (3d. ed., New York, 1949), p. 359.

41. Paul Gümmer, Note to Distler's *Choralpassion,* Cantate record T 72-083L.

42. Information from *Musik und Kirche,* V (1933), 100.

43. The first draft of this letter is in the possession of Frau Waltraut Distler, who showed it to the author.

44. Slonimsky, p. 363.

45. Draft of this letter preserved in Pastor Axel Werner Kühl's scrapbook, now located in the *Distler-Archiv,* Lübeck. Copied by the author through the gracious permission of Archivdirektor KMD Bruno Grusnick, August 1962.
46. Undated clipping in Pastor Kühl's scrapbook.
47. *Lübecker Nachrichten,* May 26, 1934 (Pastor Kühl's scrapbook).
48. Conference with Frau Distler, July 29, 1962. Yet Grabner urged Distler repeatedly in the years 1935—37 to compose for orchestra as an antidote to Distler's own feeling that he was becoming "conservative" as a composer. (Cf. Grusnick, "Hugo Distler und Hermann Grabner," p. 60 ff.)
49. Dr. Fritz Stege, "Besuch bei Hugo Distler," Kassel, newspaper clipping, [n. d.], Pastor Kühl's scrapbook.
50. Slonimsky, pp. 381—382, 384.
51. No program preserved; information from a newspaper announcement.
52. No program preserved; annotation in Pastor Kühl's scrapbook.
53. Newspaper clipping (n. d.), signed Fritz Müller, Dresden; Kühl's scrapbook.
54. "Kasseler Musiktage, 1935," *Lied und Volk,* V, No. 8 (Nov. 1935), 96.
55. Fred Hamel, "Orgelweihe in St. Jakobi," *Deutsche Allgemeine Zeitung,* Nov. 1, 1935.
56. *Musik und Kirche,* VII (1935), 286.
57. From a clipping in Pastor Kühl's scrapbook.
58. Condensed from William L. Shirer, *The Rise and Fall of the Third Reich* (New York, 1960; paperback, 1962), pp. 324—330.
59. Ursula von Rauchhaupt, p. 129. The information was given to her by Prof. Dr. Erich Thienhaus.
60. Wilhelm Stever, "Singwoche in Ratzeburg," *Musik und Kirche,* VIII (1936), 190.
61. Information from a breakfast conference with Bruno Grusnick Aug. 25, 1962, in Lübeck.
62. Erika Kienlin, "Erinnerungen an Hugo Distler," *Hausmusik,* XXII (1958), 41. All the above information is based on these reminiscences and on an unpublished letter from Frau Hellmut Typke, provided through the courtesy of Frau Waltraut Distler.
63. Slonimsky, p. 419.
64. Oskar Söhngen, *Kämpfende Kirchenmusik: Die Bewährungsprobe der evangelischen Kirchenmusik im Dritten Reich* (Kassel, 1954), p. 46. It is interesting to contrast the official "degenerate" label attached to the harpsichord concerto with Grabner's opinion, expressed in a letter of Nov. 12, 1936. "Congratulations on the *Harpsichord Concerto.* Here I see again the old 'young' Distler of the Leipzig days, with his forward-surging temperament" (Grusnick, "Hugo Distler und Hermann Grabner," 60).
65. Josef Hedar in *Sydsvenska Dagbladet Snällposten* for October 21, 1937; quoted in Söhngen, p. 45.
66. Shirer, pp. 330 f.
67. Slonimsky, p. 434.
68. Erika Kienlin, "Erinnerungen," p. 42.
69. Ibid.
70. Frau Hellmut Typke, Letter, p. 2 (Courtesy of Frau Distler).
71. Shirer, p. 331.
72. Oskar Söhngen, *Die Wiedergeburt der Kirchenmusik* (Kassel, 1953), page 158.
73. Karl-Heinrich Schweinsberg, "Hugo Distlers 'Kalendersprüche,' opus 16." *Hausmusik,* VII (1938), 107–111.

74. Hans Klotz, "Die Zweite Freiburger Orgeltagung 1938," *Musik und Kirche,* (1938), 137 ff.
75. Quoted in Söhngen, *Die Wiedergeburt,* p. 158.
76. Bruno Grusnick, "Hugo Distler zum Gedächtnis," *Lübeckische Blätter,* 1942, 18.
77. These two paragraphs are not simply the author's fancy but are based on reminiscences of Frau Waltraut Distler, July 29, 1962, Marquartstein/Obb.
78. Hans Weitzer, in *Südostdeutsche Tageszeitung,* June 29, 1939; clipping in Pastor Kühl's scrapbook.
79. Söhngen, p. 156.
80. Ibid.
81. Quoted in Gerhard Kappner, "In Memoriam Hugo Distler," *Musik und Gottedienst,* XII (1958), 83.
82. *Musik und Kirche,* XII (1940), 117.
83. Erich Schütz, *Die Musik,* XXXIII (1941), 257.
84. A page of Distler's manuscript for the second *turba* chorus was reproduced in Moser, *Die evangelische Kirchenmusik in Deutschland.* The author saw these Mss. at Frau Distler's home.
85. O. Söhngen, *Die Wiedergeburt,* p. 158.
86. Ibid.
87. Söhngen, p. 158.
88. *Musica,* VI (1952), 451.
89. H. Lehmann-Haupt, *Art Under a Dictatorship* (New York, 1954), pp. xviii–xix.
90. Freely translated from "Auf den Tod von Hugo Distler," by an unknown poet, in *Hausmusik,* XVI (1952), 155.

CHAPTER 2

THE ORGAN WORKS

It was as an organist that Hugo Distler received the major part of his musical training. He gained a fine reputation as an organ recitalist and teacher. From his contemporaries we learn further that he was an unsurpassed improviser; undoubtedly posterity is the poorer because of his rare improvisatory gift, for the most regrettable facet of the improviser's art is its total transience, unless captured by some recording device. And, as is so often the case with superb practitioners of this transient art, Distler committed to the permanence of the printed page few compositions for the organ.

In Distler's total output the organ works do not occupy the numerical percentage one might expect, considering his lifelong intimate association with this instrument. The first published works appeared in the volumes of Ramin's *Das Organistenamt*, published by Breitkopf and Härtel. The chorale prelude *Wie schön leuchtet der Morgenstern* appeared in Part II, Vol. II (p. 184), and a "Dorian Ricercare" (later incorporated in the partita on *Jesus Christus, unser Heiland*) was printed as No. 10 (pp. 80—84) in Part II, Vol. III. Both of these works were later republished by Bärenreiter in the collection of Shorter Chorale Preludes, opus 8/III.

The catalog of the organ works, all Bärenreiter publications, reads:

Two Partitas: *Nun komm, der Heiden Heiland,* opus 8/I
   Wachet auf, ruft uns die Stimme, opus 8/II
Shorter Chorale Preludes, opus 8/III
Thirty Pieces for the Small Organ or Other Keyboard Instruments,
   opus 18/I
Trio Sonata in E Minor, opus 18/II

They will be discussed in the order of publication.

Helmut Bornefeld comments that Distler's music is composed "not *for* the organ but rather *from* the organ," a distinction that makes it imperative to understand the type of instrument "from" which Distler composed this music.[1]

Two instruments, both miraculously still extant, influenced the composer deeply: the "small" organ of St. Jakobi, Lübeck, and the "house organ" built for Distler by Paul Ott of Göttingen in 1938.

When Distler became organist of St. Jakobi in 1931, the smaller of the church's two organs had the following specifications: [2]

Hauptwerk (II. Man.):	Principal 16′ (f)
	Oktave 8′ (f)
	Oktave 4′ (f)
	Oktave 2′ (f)
	Spielpfeife 8′ (mf)
	Flöte 8′ (p)
	Trommet 8′ (f)
	Mixtur (f)
Rückpositiv (I. Man.):	Gedackt 8′ (p)
	Quintatön 8′ (between p and mf)
	Hohlflöte 4′ (p)
	Prinzipal 4′ (mf)
	Oktave 2′ (between p and mf)
	Scharf (between mw and f)
	Trechterregal 8′ (between mf and p)
	Krummhorn 8′ (p)
Brustwerk (III. Man.):	Gedackt 8′ (p)
	Quintatön (p)
	Waldflöte 2′ (p)
	Zimbel (mf)
	Schalmei 8′ (p)
	Regal 8′ (p)

(The volume of this division may be somewhat decreased by closing the doors of the case.)

Pedal:	Subbass 16′ (p)
	Spielpfeifenbass 8′ (p)
	Spielpfeifenbass 4′ (p)
	Posaune 16′ (mf)
	Trommet 8′ (between mf and f)
	Trommet 4′ (between mf and p)

(The Pedal compass ranges C, D in place of C♯, E. F—d[1].)

The *Hauptwerk* and *Pedal* date from the years around 1500, built by an unknown builder; the *Brustwerk* and *Rückpositiv* were added in 1637 by the Lübeck builder, Friedrich Stellwagen.

In 1935 Distler and his brother-in-law (and former organ student), Erich Thienhaus, together with the organ builder Karl Kemper of Lübeck, drew up the following specification for the restoration of the St. Jakobi organ:

Hauptwerk:	Prinzipal 16′	Brustwerk:	Quintatön 8′
	Oktave 8′		Gedackt 4′
	Spielpfeife 8′		Waldflöte 2′
	Oktave 4′		Zimbel II
	Flöte 4′		Regal 8′
	Oktave 2′		Schalmei 4′
	Mixtur IV		
	Trommet 8′	Pedal:	Subbass 16′
Rückpositiv:	Gedackt 8′		Gadacktpommer 8′
	Quintatön 8′		Bordun 4′
	Prinzipal 4		Nachthorn 2′
	Hohlflöte 4′		Rauschpfeife IV
	Oktave 2′		Posaune 16′
	Scharf IV		Dulzian 8′
	Trechterregal 8′		Trommet 4′
	Krummhorn 8′		Regal 2′

Thus this instrument, of great tonal charm, is clearly built on the "corpus" principle, that is, with each manual division possessing a fully developed chorus, each based on a Prinzipal of different length (I: 16′; II: 4′; III: 2′), and each housed in its own functional case, with a pedal organ capable of blending with, supporting, or being heard separately from each manual division.

Distler's indebtedness to this priceless old organ was expressed in writing many times; a typical expression concerning his philosophy may be found in the preface to the *Nun komm, der Heiden Heiland* partita:

> The importance of the Baroque and pre-Baroque tonal ideal in the present and future development of organ construction, in the performing practice of the past, in the cultural revival of church music, is nowadays so generally recognized that the time appears opportune for a critical revision and appraisal of the material passed down to us, rediscovered and newly understood. In my opinion the ancient organ will only fulfill the mission which it undoubtedly owes to our time if it still proves capable

of guiding modern production to new goals and of decisively influencing it.

There are already the beginnings of a new organ music directly influenced by the past. They are few in number, however, since the only way to produce them is to acquire direct practical acquaintance with the existing technicalities and manner of performance. Further, in view of the present state of development (the limited number of old organs still to some degree intact and the scanty production of genuine new and unconventional forms of construction inspired by those of old organs) this new type of organ music can only be created by an adventurous, intensive, intentionally exclusive study of the classical type of organ. The present chorale partitas owe their origin, form, principle, and justification for existence to long years of experience which the good fortune of being custodian to the old St. Jakobi organ in Lübeck allowed me to acquire.[3]

Partita, Nun komm, der Heiden Heiland, opus 8/I

The partita *Nun komm, der Heiden Heiland*, opus 8/I, is dedicated to the composer's teacher, Hermann Grabner. The work is in four main sections: Toccata, Chorale with Variations, Chaconne, and Toccata. The melody *Nun komm, der Heiden Heiland* is that of Martin Luther's chorale, a Germanization of St. Ambrose's Advent hymn *Veni, Redemptor gentium,* and the melody is pre-Reformation, based on Gregorian chant.

Just how literally to incorporate a cantus firmus melody in a composition is one of the most perplexing problems confronting the contemporary composer. Distler's work uses the chorale melody as the melodic basis for composition, and he also bases the harmonic material on the most prominent interval in the chorale, the perfect fourth heard at the very incipit:

Ex. 1.

Nun komm, der Hei - den   Hei - land,

This interval is clearly outstanding in the otherwise stepwise first phrase. Distler's Toccata is thoroughly dominated by the perfect fourth. Opening with a pedal solo in which this interval is often heard, the brief movement continues with an upward flurry over a tonic pedal point:

Ex. 2. P. 4, Score 5.

A sequence based on fourths leads to rapid parallel fourths, still over the tonic pedal. At the beginning of the last line the other interval that is to be prominent in the partita, the minor seventh, is heard melodically (still with the two manual voices in parallel fourths):

Ex. 3. P. 5, Score 3.

A succinct indication of the solid basis for Distler's organ style in the traditions of the late Renaissance is the incorporation of Balthasar Resinarius' harmonization of the chorale without any feeling of stylistic disunity. Seven separate variations follow the simple 4-part statement of the theme.

Variation 1 is a Bicinium, a form not often found in organ literature since Bach! Reminiscent even more of the earlier masters such as Sweelinck, this movement offers the phrases of the chorale alternating with a countersubject based on this rhythmic pattern:

Ex. 4. P. 6, Score 3.

A mistake in the first score, left hand, of the printed edition should be noted. Obviously the two notes following the eighth rest should be barred as sixteenths (as above), not as eighths. The fact that the Bicinium is not barred in measures might make this error somewhat more difficult to spot, especially in reading the work. Another possible printing error may be in the first statement of the rhythmic countersubject in the right hand, which has the group of four sixteenths printed thus:

Ex. 5. P. 6, Score 3.

rather than with a G as above. When this same turn reappears at the end of the variation, the G is employed. Distler does often change the patterns in his compositions ever so slightly, perhaps in deference to the artistic principle, noted by Renoir, that "Nature abhors symmetry, preferring balance." The author, with this in mind, prefers to accept the printed B-flat in this case. Final proof is impossible, for the manuscript of this work was burned in the bombing of Kassel during World War II.

Variation 2 is a trio with two freely imitative voices over the cantus, which is played on an 8-foot stop in the pedal. Variation 3 is a solo for a reed color (specified as Schalmey 8′) with tremulant; Variation 4 a leggiero manual variation in which the cantus is heard in the lowest sustained notes of the left hand, and to which the shimmering Cymbal mixture adds a lightness and brilliance that suits the writing. This is a particularly fine example of the way in which the composition stems *from* the instrument. The fourth and the fifth, its harmonic inversion, are given continued prominence:

Ex. 6. P. 11, Score 1.

Variation 5 features a favorite Distler rhythmic motive in the pedal:

This rhythmic device, used five times in this variation, outlines, each time, the minor seventh.

In Variation 6 the right hand has rapid figurations, again outlining the fourth while the pedal and left hand present the cantus firmus in canon at the twelfth. The 7th, and last, variation presents a florid coloration of the melody against an accompaniment that at times punctuates the floridity with sharp anacrustic, trumpet-like effects. The variation ends with a *tierce de picardy*.

The Chaconne bass is the opening phrase of the chorale:

Ex. 7. P. 18, M. 1.

It consists of 18 variations, each growing in intensity and complexity of registration. After a rhythmic crescendo through the introduction successively of sixteenth notes in pairs, triplets, triplets with dotted eighth notes: ♩ 𝅘𝅥 𝅘𝅥𝅮 , triplets containing pairs of sixteenths: ♩ 𝅘𝅥𝅮 𝅘𝅥 , and variation of color by dialogs between two manuals, the pedal breaks into a virtuoso passage in sixteenth notes at Variation 10.

At Variation 13 brilliant passage work for the manuals begins in one voice; Variation 14 transfers this same passagework to the left hand, with staccato fourths for the top voice; after both hands continue with sixteenth notes, the 16th variation features intervals, largely sevenths and fourths, alternating between the two hands. A heavily dotted rhythm punctuates the 17th variation, while the 18th, in reality a coda, features a buildup of sound effected through the use of double pedal, one voice of which is a tonic pedal point.

An exact repetition of the opening Toccata brings this first Distler organ work to a brilliant conclusion.

Partita, Wachet auf, ruft uns die Stimme, opus 8/II

The partita on *Wachet auf* was written in 1935 when this chorale seems particularly to have excited the composer's imagination: the motet on this chorale also dates from this year. It was a further ". . . attempt toward a fruitful interpretation for present-day composition of the old Baroque and pre-Baroque tonal ideals of the organ and of the appropriate forms issuing therefrom," [4] as Distler wrote in his preface to the Bärenreiter Edition. Where the earlier Partita *Nun komm, der Heiden Heiland* might be considered "absolute" music insofar as it did not attempt a verse by verse portrayal of the chorale text, or for that matter, word painting in general, the second partita might be viewed as a bit of program music, its three sections portraying clearly the three consecutive moods of the chorale's three stanzas: the watchmanlike, trumpeting spirit of Stanza 1, the receptive mood of Zion's hearing the summons, expressed in Stanza 2, and, finally, the dancelike, lively joy of the redeemed in the fugal Stanza 3.[5]

In analyzing Distler's use of thematic material in his second partita, we find that all the chorale phrases are completely stated in the first section of the work, the Toccata.[6] This movement begins with a rapidly rising manual flurry, in canon for 15 notes:

Ex. 8. P. 4, M. 1.

The pedal sounds its first "trumpet call" in measure three, elaborating this motive twice before the actual chorale theme enters in measure seven; above this melody, in measure eight, the opening flurry is heard again with the same short canonic treatment which opened the Toccata.

The second phrase is expanded considerably; the composer seems loathe to leave the top C of the phrase, but finally, after nine measures of increasingly agitated rocking back and forth from G to C, the phrase triumphantly descends.

Ex. 9. P. 6, Mm. 6-7.

In keeping with the original *Barform* (AAB) of the chorale, there is an exact repetition of the material just presented, to form the second of the "zwei Stollen." (AA)

At the end of this repetition a toccata-like flourish in the manual leads to the next section.

Ex. 10. P. 8, Mm. 6-7.

The chorale melody is now heard in the soprano in a phrase played on the *Rückpositiv;* this phrase is echoed immediately on the *Brustwerk,* with the accompanying figure moved up a fourth and altered. The same treatment is given the next melodic fragment, to which a sequence is added.

The sixth phrase ("Hallelujah") enters in the pedal, and is imitated at the fifth by the left hand, playing on the *Hauptwerk.*

Ex. 11. P. 9, M. 2.

The seventh and eighth phrases are treated in the same canonic way; the final phrase is an ecstatic coloratura in the soprano over a descending pedal; with the tempo indication "Broadly, but mightily excited; hymnlike," the first verse concludes.

Ex. 12. P. 9, M. 6.

Verse II, a Bicinium, presents the entire cantus firmus again, in readily recognizable form. This movement is also in *Barform,* in a sort of free double counterpoint. The most striking characteristic of this movement is a feature that became increasingly typical of Distler's instrumental style: great complexity of microrhythmic subdivisions. The nervous and vital effects thus achieved, so reminiscent of the birdcall derivatives of Olivier Messiaen, delicately and individually embellish the chorale melody.[7]

After three measures (one in 4/4, one in 3/2, another in 4/4) of this nervous embellishment in one voice, the cantus is introduced, preferably by a soft reed voice, such as the Vox Humana.

Ex. 13. P. 10, Mm. 4-5.

When this phrase is repeated to complete the *Barform,* the cantus is placed above the contrapuntal associate, making true double invertible counterpoint.

The third section, marked "almost twice as quickly," is marked by an intensification of effect, gained by a melodic ostinato figure, and an increase of the number of voices to four, two of them consisting of C pedal points, one above, and one below the two active voices.

Ex. 14. P. 11, M. 10.

The effectiveness of this Bicinium is based so firmly on the conception of rhythm "as melody deprived of its pitch," [8] that two quotations, one from Dame Edith Sitwell, and one from the composer himself, suggested themselves as appendages to the factual discussion of the composition.

"Rhythm," wrote Edith Sitwell, "is one of the principal translators between dream and reality. Rhythm might be described as, to the world of sound, what light is to the world of sight. It shapes and gives meaning." [9]

From Distler:

> Rhythm is for us no longer an unbound genius, an often-furious outbreaking expression of power, but rather — somewhat in the sense of the old Netherlandish-northern Polyrhythms — an expression of the independence (one might say: the ability to answer for its being) of the structure itself, with the aim: an increase in the great total architectural effect.[10]

The Fugue (Verse III) bears the tempo indication "Very quickly, almost dancelike," and the 13-bar 3/8 subject bears out this suggested mood:

Ex. 15. P. 12, Mm. 1-13.

Six sections are indicated by double barlines in this 4-voice fugue. At the fourth section the movement develops into more of a fantasia than a strict fugue, but the first sections are securely grounded in fugal techniques.

The subject is heard successively in each of the four voices in the first section in the sequence soprano, alto, tenor, and bass. The answers are tonal; one false entry occurs in the alto between the tenor and bass entries, and the bass entry is shortened to seven measures of the subject with a cadential formula of three measures.

After an episode (manualiter), the first two phrases of the cantus firmus are introduced simultaneously against the fugue subject and contrapuntal associates. Closing the first section of the Fugue, the third phrase enters in soprano and pedal simultaneously.

In section two the first three phrases of the chorale are repeated against the fugue subject (the influence of the *Barform* again). This section is played entirely on the manuals.

Ex. 16. P. 14, Mm. 20-24; p. 15, Mm. 3-4.

Section three introduces phrases four and five, and, in the fragmentation of these motives, leads to the toccata-like fourth section. This bravura writing conceals the outline of the sixth phrase.[11]

Ex. 17. P. 17, Mm. 13-14.

Phrase seven is introduced in the pedal at the end of this section, with the eighth phrase in octaves against it.

Section five, of only two measures, presents the last phrase of the chorale in the soprano against coloration in the tenor and a descending pedal line, while the sixth and final section is also based on this final phrase, presented in trill-like manual figurations over a tonic pedal point.

One German writer lamented the fact that Distler never wrote a strictly constructed fugue, à la Reger.[12] But why, indeed, should he have done so? What Reger did had been done; none could possibly have surpassed him in his own style. What Distler did, instead, was to integrate, with great technical skill and great élan, the chorale melody into a composition that expresses joyfully the moods of the chorale texts.

What more jubilant expression could one imagine than Distler's dance-like fugal movement for the stirring words:

Every soul in Thee rejoices;
From men and from angelic voices
Be glory given to Thee alone!
Now the gates of pearl receive us,
Thy presence never more shall leave us,
We stand with angels round Thy throne.
Earth cannot give below
The bliss Thou dost bestow.
Alleluia!
Grant us to raise,
To length of days,
The triumph-chorus of Thy praise.[13]

If Distler had not written any other organ compositions, this one partita would insure him a place in the history of composition for the instrument. It remains a unique "sermon in tone," a superb expression of the short-lived evangelical revival in Germany between the two world wars.

Kleine Orgelchoral-Bearbeitungen, opus 8/III

In this collection of compositions dating from his days as organist of St. Jakobi, Distler presented chorale preludes and new harmonizations of the chorales for seven widely used Lutheran hymns. These compositions, undoubtedly based on Distler's highly acclaimed improvised preludes to the singing of the chorales at St. Jakobi, offered organ works somewhat less challenging than the two partitas to those desiring new music born of the organ building ideals fostered by the *Orgelbewegung*. Distler stated in his preface to this collection that the chorale harmonizations included were not to be considered mandatory, but were to serve as guides to the possibilities of free harmonizations for these time-honored melodies.

Number one treats the Epiphany chorale *Wie schön leuchtet der Morgenstern*. The cantus firmus is presented, with some alterations, in the tenor, throughout this 2-page composition. The interval of the fourth is prominent in the contrapuntal associate woven about the tune, and the harmonic interval of the perfect fourth is also prominent in Distler's treatment of this chorale.

Ex. 18. P. 4, Mm. 1-5.

Second is the New Year's chorale *Das alte Jahr vergangen ist.* Similar in spirit to the Bach treatment of this chorale in the *Orgelbüchlein* is the chromaticism and the melismatic character of the soprano line. But, whereas Bach places the ornamented cantus firmus in the soprano, Distler's soprano is a free melody, and the cantus is in the alto voice, which together with the third voice is to be played on a reed (the *Brustwerk* Regal 8′ with optional tremulant is suggested).

Ex. 19. P. 7, Mm. 1-2.

Third is a 3-section partita on the Communion chorale *Jesus Christus, unser Heiland, der von uns den Gotteszorn wandt.* Consisting of Chorale, Bicinium, and Fugue, this is the most extended work to be found in opus 8/III. The Bicinium presents Distler's customary complex rhythmic subdivisions, but, instead of double counterpoint, the cantus firmus is retained in the lower voice throughout, with the coloratura upper voice (assigned to a 4-foot flute with optional tremulant) embellishing this steady cantus with its birdlike cantillation.

The Fugue offers measures of varying lengths: the first section, for example has two in 4/4, one in 5/4, two more in 4/4, one in 5/4, two in 4/4, one in 3/4, one in 4/4, and three in 3/4. This 3-voice fugue has the sturdy incipit of the chorale as its theme:

Ex. 20. P. 12, Mm. 1-4.

The exposition is followed by a *Brustwerk* section with doubled tempo. Next comes a triple-time mutation of the theme with an interesting play between three and two in the later measures:

Ex. 21. P. 14, Mm. 15-16; p. 15, Mm. 1-4.

The Fugue (and the partita) concludes with a toccata-figured flourish suggesting a written-out set of baroque embellishments, complete with final mordent in parallel fourths.

Next, three preludes to the traditional Lutheran Agnus Dei, *Christe, du Lamm Gottes.*

Ex. 22. P. 18, Mm. 1-2.

The first prelude presents the cantus in the alto, with a 3-note ostinato figure in the pedal, with an open-sounding registration: flutes 16′ and 4′.

Ex. 23. P. 18, M. 1.

The second, also only one page in length, has the melody in canon at the twelfth between pedal and alto; the soprano begins as a repetition of the soprano from the preceding prelude, a fourth lower, but does not continue with an exact repetition beyond the second measure.

The third prelude begins like the first and observes this exact copying for three measures. It continues in a similar vein, with an extension of the cadential material.

Fifth is a treatment of the Easter chorale *Mit Freuden zart.* Beginning quietly as a trio (with a brief imitative entry — canon at the octave between left hand and pedal) this grows in volume and in rhythmic intensity, first by the introduction of triplets, and then by the use of a melismatic tenor with subdivisions into seven thirty-second notes.

Ex. 24. P. 22, Mm. 1-3.

manual
pedal

Number six, on the chorale for "Totensonntag" *Ach wie flüchtig, ach wie nichtig,* is a 1-page gem. The cantus is heard first in the tenor, is then transferred to the alto, and returns to the tenor again for the conclusion of the work. Sadness is suggested through an extreme use of chromaticism, and a pedal motive of dotted eighth and sixteenth notes, followed by the downward interval of an octave, pervades the slow-moving setting:

Ex. 25. P. 25, Mm. 1-2.

The final chorale to be treated in this set is the vesper hymn *Christ, der du bist der helle Tag.* This chorale also receives a 3-section partita (Chorale, Bicinium, and Pastorale).

The opening chorale, to be played on the *Rückpositiv* 8′ Quin-tatön, keeps the cantus firmus in the soprano and features irregular alternation between 2/2 and 3/2 meters.

The Bicinium has the cantus alternating between the two voices, but the contrapuntal associate is a free one. The Bicinium concludes with the addition of two voices, a pedal point and its inversion, a device which Distler also used in the Bicinium of the *Wachet auf* partita.

The appellation "Pastorale" tells little about the final movement of this partita. The three manual voices begin imitatively (see below, Ex. 26), after which the pedal sounds forth the theme in a syncopated rhythm (Ex. 27).

Ex. 26. P. 29, Mm. 1-4.

Ex. 27. P. 29, Mm. 3-7.

The work ends, customarily enough, with a flourish over a double pedal point.

Dreissig Spielstücke für die Kleinorgel oder andere Tasteninstrumente, opus 18/I

When Distler left Lübeck because of the worsening conditions surrounding church music, he also left his treasured instrument, the "small" organ of St. Jakobi. With no church position to provide him with a practice instrument in Stuttgart, it became increasingly desirable that he purchase a house organ. The instrument he ordered from Paul Ott, organ builder of Göttingen, had the following specifications:

Unterwerk:	Lieblich Gedackt 8′
	Prinzipal 4′
	Waldflöte 2′
	Nasat 2⅔′
	Zimbel II-III rks.
Oberwerk:	Regal 8′
	Gedacktflöte 4′
	Prinzipal 2′
	Sifflöte 1′
	Terz 1⅗′
	Quinte 1⅓′
Pedal:	Dulzian 16′
	Pommer 8′
	Rohrgedackt 4′
	Rauschpfeife II rks.

Mechanical action, slider chests, manual coupler, two pedal couplers, tremulant, Dulzian enclosed; *Oberwerk* enclosed.[14]

Distler was highly influenced by the intimate charm of this instrument. His *Nachwort* to the *Spielstücke* begins,

93

The present collection will encourage the reinstitution of the organ as a household instrument. In range, technique, form, and content, the thirty little pieces clearly exhibit their intimate purpose. They are intended neither for concert nor for church performance, but rather to inspire pleasure in music-making at home. They modestly endeavour to contribute to making the house organ and small organ also once again instrumental in creating music the source of which is rooted in national life, home music-making, recreation and festivity. As the meaning and task of all music-making at home and in social gatherings has been, or at least should have been, to lift us out of the workaday world, to enrich it again relatively, to truly "sanctify" it, the organ in particular could in this connection play a specifically important role now and in the future.[15]

These compositions, some not more than a single page in length, are not titled, and no suggested registrations are provided. However, in the *Nachwort* the composer has suggested the formal plans which he had in mind when composing the collection. The first four pieces may be played together to form a sonatina.

Number one (marked "fast quarter-notes") is a toccata-like intonation a single page in length:

Ex. 28. P. 2, M. 1.

Number two, a concertino, to be played in the same tempo as the first, has a toccata-like "B" section, which leads to a recapitulation of the first theme and a 3-measure coda.

Ex. 29. P. 3, Mm. 1-3.

Ex. 30. P. 3, M. 22; p. 4, Mm. 1-2.

The third piece, a small chaconne, begins thus:

Ex. 31. P. 6, Mm. 1-6.

Above this 5-measure, overlapping bass, Distler has composed 16 variations. At the fourth recurrence of the theme, the bass is filled in with sixteenth notes, at the sixth the theme is changed to major and placed in the soprano, at the seventh, the theme is placed in the tenor, the former counterpoint is placed above it, and a third voice is added; the major section is continued through variation 11; variations 11 through 16 are a repetition of the opening variations, completing the arch form of the composition.

Four is a canon at the octave, and it completes the suggested sonatina.

Ex. 32. P. 9, Mm. 1-8.

Five, a single page in A Minor, with the superscription "Slow whole notes" (in 4/2 meter) stands alone. Number six, also in A Minor, is a toccata that may be used in combination with number seven, a fugato:

Ex. 33. P. 14, Mm. 1-3.

An optional ending is provided for a return to number six, and the composer has also suggested that only the final six measures of the preceding toccata might also serve as an ending, if both pieces are played together.

Number eight is again an ABA composition, with the "B" section in 5/8 meter. Number nine is a gentle fantasy of a single page; number ten, a pastorale, reminiscent of a shepherd's pipe:

Ex. 34. P. 19, Mm. 1-2.

Numbers 12 through 30 consist of three sets of variations, each of which, however, may be played separately. The first set of variations is based on the folksong *Frisch auf, gut Gsell, lass rummer gahn.*

Ex. 35. P. 21, Mm. 1-5.

Five straightforward variations are included in this first set; the second is an inversion of the theme statement; variation four is a 1-page toccata; and the fifth concludes with a double pedal point and mordent written out, two features typical of Distler's keyboard writing.

96

The second set of variations, based on the tune *Elselein, liebstes Elselein* from the *Glogauer Liederbuch* of 1480, consists of a theme, five variations, and an ornamented repetition of the theme. These variations are more fanciful than the preceding set. The theme ending with the "Landini" cadence typical of the period, is followed by a favorite

Ex. 36. P. 27, Mm. 1-4.

Distler treatment, a Bicinium, in which the theme appears in the left hand accompanied by this rhythmic pattern in the right:

Ex. 37. P. 27, (No. 19), Mm. 1-3.

The repetition of the theme with ornamentation written out in the alto and bass voices is reminiscent of the Renaissance colorist masters such as Hofhaimer and Ammerbach.

Ex. 38. P. 34, Mm. 1-4.

The final set of variations is based on Hans Leo Hassler's harmonization of the tune *Wo Gott zum Haus nit gibt sein Gunst* (1608):

97

Ex. 39. P. 34, (No. 25), Mm. 1-3.

The first variation, again a Bicinium, presents the phrases of the tune in alternation between right and left hands with a contrapuntal associate. The second variation, more quiet, presents the theme in the lowest voice, transposed to B-flat. In the third variation the theme is heard in the lowest notes of a series of toccata-like arpeggios. The fourth variation features shorter note values in the bass part, and the thirtieth *Spielstück,* a return of the theme, simply harmonized, is somewhat reminiscent of the final chorale prelude of Brahms's opus 121 in its use of an echo at the end of each phrase.

Orgelsonate (Trio), opus 18/II

Distler's final composition for the organ, the Trio Sonata, was a further outgrowth of the influence of his house organ and his love of chamber music, as well as a reflection of his great love for the Bach works in this same trio idiom. The trio is the supreme possibility for the organ, a form in which each hand may be independently engaged on a separate manual while the feet are also independently active with a bass part for the pedals. Since Bach's death and the decline of polyphonic music this medium, so ideally suited to the organ, has not often been utilized.

The Trio Sonata in E Minor was composed in Stuttgart in 1939 and is dedicated to Distler's brother-in-law, Erich Thienhaus, who had helped plan the specifications of the house organ. Formally the work offers nothing radically new or different. The first movement is in Sonata-Allegro form. The theme is buoyant and energetic:

Ex. 40. P. 5, Mm. 1-8.

A countersubject is heard immediately against the theme, first in the pedal:

Ex. 41. P. 5, Mm. 2-5.

The theme is repeated immediately in the right hand as a real answer, with the countersubject in the left hand against it; a shortened entry of the theme in the pedal (key of the subdominant) leads to a double bar, which signifies the beginning of the development. The theme is spun out, lengthened, fragmented, as this example from the very beginning of the development illustrates:

Ex. 42. P. 5, M. 18; p. 6, Mm. 1-5.

A sequential section of the development is built over a chromatic pedal line, reminiscent of a Baroque chaconne bass:

Ex. 43. P. 7, Mm. 5-13.

A 6-measure cadenza leads to the recapitulation, an exact repetition of the exposition; this is followed by a coda, which begins

Ex. 44. P. 9, Mm. 16-18.

This "rocking" figuration continues for 11 more measures over the dominant pedal point; with a piling-up of the perfect-fourth

99

motive in stretto in all three voices, the first movement is brought to an end on an *E* in all voices, the utmost simplicity.

The second movement begins with a free toccata of nine measures, after which a simple aria, built largely on the interval of the minor seventh, proceeds to a gentle conclusion,

Ex. 45. P. 11, Mm. 10-12.

in G major.

The third movement is somewhat more unusual in form. Titled simply *III. Recht geschwinde Achtel* ("Quickly moving eighths"), it begins with a fanfare-like theme (A):

Ex. 46. P. 14, Mm. 1-6.

after which the main theme of the movement is heard (B):

Ex. 47. P. 14, Mm. 20-23; p. 15, Mm. 1-3.

The development of this "B" theme, finally extended and heard in octaves between left hand and pedal, leads to a recapitulation of "A". A slightly more quiet section (C) is distinctive for its lack of 16′ pedal sound:

Ex. 48. P. 17, Mm. 11-13.

A short toccata section leads gradually to the main tempo, and the "A" theme again:

Ex. 49. P. 18, Mm. 22-25.

The "B" theme, in 3/4 meter rather than the former 3/8, is then used as a bass for a short chaconne with five variations. The work concludes with the piling-up of motives so dear to Distler, over a tonic pedal. The final two measures are quoted to show the effect he achieves with these techniques and the triple mordent on the final chord.

Ex. 50. P. 24, Mm. 9-10.

The form of this final movement might be considered to be a rondo: ABACAB Chaconne, Coda, or, possibly, a large ABA form with this grouping: A   B   A   .
                                        AB   AC   AB(Coda)

The registration suggested by Distler in his preface to the Trio Sonata tells much about the character of the music:

> The registration should be in the chamber music style; not too brittle and jingly, but rather somewhat bold, especially in the finale. The middle movement permits the use of the tremulant, even in the toccata-like introduction, which is to be registered quite glitteringly (possibly with a delicate Zimbel). In the trio of the finale the left hand and pedal are accompanimental. The little chaconne at the end can be registered a bit stronger than the principal theme.[16]

With this cheerful work, expressive of the peace and happiness he felt in Stuttgart, Distler brought his organ composition to a close. That he should have chosen a form that is in itself a tribute to Bach once again showed his close ties with the past, ties which are evident throughout his creations for the organ.

The forms in which Distler wrote — chorale preludes and partitas, toccatas, chaconnes, variations, and bicinia — he copied from the most distinguished era of organ composition, and he endowed them with new life and new devices. His choice of modal themes and his lessening thereby of the power of the leading tone was again a renewal of something old, but a presentation of something quite new and different to the organists of his generation. The fact that he could incorporate harmonizations by Resinarius and Hassler into his own compositions without any feeling of stylistic disunity proves just how close in spirit Distler's organ works are to the 16th century.

Distler's use of a linear style, a polyphonic treatment of themes, is a most prominent feature of his organ works. To this linear treatment he brought new rhythmic vitality: in toccata-like, improvisatory sections of his works he eschewed completely the use of bar lines. His use of highly complex subdivisions of the beat, of repeated melodic and rhythmic patterns reminiscent of birdsong, and of occasional asymmetric meters (5/4) gives his music the most highly rhythmic character of any German organ music of his generation.

A delicacy of texture, demonstrated by a frequent use of counterpoint in only two voices, and a careful specification of the exact registrations desired showed organists of his time new roads to follow. Helmut Bornefeld comments, "Distler's Lübeck registrations [i. e., for the St. Jakobi organ] were a revelation to a whole generation of organists and did more toward the shaping of a new organistic tonal knowledge than whole books of theoretical writing."[17]

The organ works of Hugo Distler, while few in number, form an important chapter in the history of composition for the instrument; his maturity at the very beginning of the *Orgelbewegung* and his natural affinity for the polyphonic schools of composition dictated the shape of his output. As the first young 20th-century composer to write specifically for the *Werkorgel,* or instrument built on the division principle, he might be considered the founder of a school of composition that is still flourishing.

1. Helmut Bornefeld, *Orgelbau und neue Orgelmusik* (Kassel, 1952), p. 14.
2. Specifications, with volume indications of the various ranks, printed in the published score of the partita *Nun komm, der Heiden Heiland.*
3. Preface to Bärenreiter Edition 637. English edition; no translator credited.
4. Preface to Bärenreiter Edition 883; translated by Philip Gehring.
5. This association with text is suggested in the article by Werner Bieske, "Die Orgelwerke Hugo Distlers," *Musik und Kirche,* XXII (1952), pp. 177–181.
6. The analysis of this partita is based, in part, on George Klump's "A Brief Analysis of the Partita *Wachet auf*" by Hugo Distler, program notes to Eastman School of Music Lecture Recital, August 4, 1961.
7. Although Messiaen and Distler were born in the same year, it is doubtful that Distler knew of Messiaen's work; at any rate this feature of Messiaen's writing is a later development. Distler's use of these effects was, so far as the author can determine, an original device.
8. Description of rhythm by Schopenhauer, mentioned by Edith Sitwell. Possibly she has reference to his words: "Das rhythmische Element ist das wesentlichste; da es, für sich allein und ohne das andere, eine Art Melodie darzustellen vermag . . ." (Schopenhauer, *Schriften über Musik im Rahmen seiner Aesthetik,* ed. Karl Stabenow [Regensburg, 1922], p. 139.)
9. Edith Sitwell, "Some Notes on my own Poetry," *Collected Poems of Edith Sitwell* (New York, 1954), p. xv.
10. Hugo Distler, "Worte," *Musica,* VI (1952), 453.
11. So well concealed, in fact, is the sixth phrase that Klump in his analysis states that it is missing entirely. This seemed rather strange since the entire chorale had been included in each of the other movements; a perusal of the shape of the toccata-figures revealed the melody, just barely hidden.
12. Wilhelm Stahl, *Musikgeschichte Lübecks* (Kassel, 1952), II, 184: "Ueberhaupt suchen wir bei dem jüngeren Meister vergeblich nach einer regelrechten, streng durchgeführten Fuge."
13. Translated from Phillip Nicolai by Francis Crawford Burkitt for the *English Hymnal* (1906), (2d ed., London, 1933), p. 12.
14. These specifications are printed in the *Nachwort* to the *Dreissig Spielstücke,* Bärenreiter Edition 1288. The author saw this instrument, now housed in the St. Jürgenkapelle, Ratzeburger Allee, Lübeck. A Subbass 16' has been added to the *Pedal,* and a Gedacktpommer 8' to the *Oberwerk.*
15. *Nachwort* (Notes), Bärenreiter Edition 1288; no translator credited.
16. Translated by Philip Gehring.
17. Helmut Bornefeld, "Orgelbau und neue Orgelmusik," p. 15; translated by Philip Gehring.

CHAPTER 3

SACRED CHORAL WORKS

The central position in Distler's creative output, both in quantity and importance, belongs to his compositions for choral ensembles. This was indeed a refreshing change and a rather startling one, as Oskar Söhngen points out:

> He and other composers of his generation brought to an end the undisputed reign of instrumental music, which characterized the 19th and early 20th century, through the rediscovery of the human voice, and of its marvellous, mysterious, and plastic qualities. Music-making thereby acquired a fresh significance and aim. Because the voice is bound to the word, the burden of the words assumes paramount importance, and vocal music more than any other has the capacity to convey this. Weary of the orgy of continually changing orchestral color, weary also of its own image which suited the music of the *fin de siècle*, the new style of vocal music turned to some event, some message of which it wished to sing and speak. For Hugo Distler this was, first and foremost, the message of the Gospel. He wished to spread it abroad through his music as a declaration, as sermon, song of praise, and as a proclamation. Thus his music is governed essentially by the text; the words kindle his creative imagination and control the formal aspect of his compositions. Not, to be sure, the word in its immediately obvious or literal sense; one will search in vain in Distler's music for illustrative touches, devices of tone coloring, or expressions of "Affekt." His concern is always with the meaning behind the words, with the spirit and feeling of them which he brings out in his music. Distler's musical language dematerializes the words in order to liberate *The Word*, and thereby to explain it at the same time. And Distler is a preacher of impressive earnestness and consuming witness. One can hardly fail to be affected by the forcefulness of his musical preaching.
>
> There is another element which bears upon the understanding of his music. In choral works, the singer places himself consciously in partnership with others. "It is certainly not by chance,"

Hugo Distler once wrote, "that the new German music, and church music in particular, is primarily choral music. The very cultivation of choral music put an end to that harmful gap between performers and listeners which had opened in the course of the previous century." Like many others, Distler had appreciated the isolation and the needs of creative men, but at the same time he knew that his music could fulfill its message and have its effect only in the service of the community. Hence the hymn, together with Bible texts, plays an important part in his creative work.[1]

From his student days in Leipzig, when he conducted the *Sportklub* chorus, through the Lübeck years with his St. Jakobi *Kantorei* choirs and his participation in the *Sing- und Spielkreis* Distler was always associated with choral groups as conductor and singer. The deciding factor which led him to accept the position at the *Hochschule* in Stuttgart was the promise of a fine choral ensemble, and we have already seen how he immediately formed the *Esslinger Singakademie* for the performance of larger choral works. His success as a choral conductor in the Festival of German Choral Music at Graz led to his appointment in Berlin, and less than a year before his death he assumed the high position of conductor of the Berlin *Staats- und Domchor*. Through countless choral workshops and *Singwochen* Distler spread his distinctive choral art; it could scarcely be disputed that he brought great practical knowledge to his composition for the vocal medium.

From his Leipzig compositions, influenced by hearing the superb *Thomanerchor* of men and boys, conducted by Professor Karl Straube, and written because of this influence for large ensemble combinations (six parts for one, a double chorus for another), it is interesting to note the change in employment of forces when Distler was faced by a small children's choir, or by an inadequate volunteer group. His compositions from the early Lübeck years are for 3-part combinations, either for three higher voices, or, occasionally for two women's voices and one part for the men.

During the years in which he was actively associated with church music, that is, particularly until he left St. Jakobi in Lübeck (April 1937), Distler created primarily for the church, as a survey of his work will show. Once again the music will be discussed in its order of publication.

Opus 2   Motette über den Choral "Herzlich lieb hab' ich dich, o Herr"

Opus 3   Eine deutsche Choralmesse

Opus 4   Kleine Adventsmusik

Opus 5   Der Jahrkreis

Opus 6/I   Kleine geistliche Abendmusik: "Christ, der du bist der helle Tag"

Opus 6/II Drei Choralmotetten

Opus 7   Choralpassion

(Opus 8, it will be remembered, comprised the sacred organ works.)

Opus 10   Die Weihnachtsgeschichte

Opus 11   Choralkantate, "Wo Gott zum Haus nit gibt sein Gunst"

           Choralkantate, "Nun danket all und bringet Ehr"

Opus 12   Geistliche Chormusik

Opus 13   Liturgische Sätze

(In addition to these works with assigned opus numbers there are a number of shorter choral works, most of them based on chorales.)

Motet, Herzlich lieb hab' ich dich, o Herr, opus 2

This motet, Distler's first published choral composition, already shows an absolute mastery of the polyphonic idiom and reveals as well many of the devices that were to become idiomatic with the composer. It is based on the chorale *Herzlich lieb hab' ich dich, o Herr,* text by Martin Schalling (1532—1608), set to a melody dated "before 1577." This melody is familiar as the closing chorale of Bach's *St. John Passion,* which uses the text of the third stanza, *Ach Herr, lass dein lieb' Engelein.*

Ex. 51. P. 3, Score 1.

The motet, in three stanzas, like the chorale, begins with a movement for double choir (eight parts). The chorale melody is heard, with slight ornamentation, first in the soprano of the first chorus; for the repetition of this melodic phrase, it is transferred to the alto of the first chorus. The chorale remains primarily with the first chorus throughout the movement while the second chorus echoes fragments first heard in the first group. An interesting and stylistic use of the two choirs is illustrated in the answering back and forth of the words, *mein Teil, mein Trost.*

Ex. 52. P. 11, M. 2.

mein Teil, mein Trost, mein Teil, mein Trost, mein Teil___

The second stanza ("Truly, Lord, my body and soul are Thy gift to me") is set for single choir of five parts (divided alto) and soprano obbligato solo. This soprano solo is a recitation of Psalm 18 ("I love Thee, O Lord, my Strength"), set to the seventh Gregorian Psalm tone. With the chorale melody in the soprano of the chorus, it blends beautifully:

Ex. 53. P. 14, Mm. 1-6.

Above the closing words of this stanza ("Lord Jesus Christ, my God and Lord") the soloist intones the liturgically proper ending for a psalm, the Gloria Patri; a melismatic Amen, of which so many examples are to be found in Distler's later works, ends this second stanza.

The third stanza, again for double chorus, assigns the chorale to the second choir while the first develops the plaintive call *Ach Herr*. The closing section of the motet is a fugue, which builds to a full 8-part climax.

Ex. 54. P. 25, Mm. 6-9.

Als-dann vom Tod er- wek – ke mich, er – wek –ke

The solo soprano is heard again in a freely melismatic line above an 8-part accompaniment:

Ex. 55. P. 32, Mm. 1-3.

Ich will dich prei - sen   ,   prei –   –
–   –   – sen e   –   wig lich

The motet concludes softly with repetitions of the word *ewiglich* ("eternally"). Published by Breitkopf and Härtel late in 1930 on the recommendation of Thomaskantor Karl Straube and dedicated to Distler's friend Olaf Fröisland, who died on Oct. 25, 1929, in Haganik, this work is indeed an impressive opus 2.

Eine deutsche Choralmesse, opus 3

Distler's first Lübeck composition is, fittingly enough, dedicated to Bruno Grusnick, the founder and conductor of the *Sing- und Spielkreis*, in which Distler himself sang, and the group which first performed most of his sacred works.

The first hearing of this German Mass was an event of the *Nordisch-deutsche Orgelwoche* on Oct. 4, 1931. It was published in March 1932 by Breitkopf and Härtel of Leipzig.

Distler has scored this work for a 6-part choir: two sopranos, alto, tenor, and two basses. Each of the five sections is based on a chorale from the 16th century: I. Kyrie is based on a Madgeburg *Kyrie, Gott, aller Welt Schöpfer* of 1545; II. Magnificat is based on a chorale of the Bohemian Brethren, 1566; III. Credo is also based on a chorale of the Bohemian Brethren; IV. The Words of Institution use Martin Luther's *Verba testamenti* from the *Deutsche Messe* of 1526 and a chorale *(Als Jesus Christus, unser Herr, wusst, dass sein Zeit nun kommen wär)* from Veit Dietrich's *Abendbüchlein* of 1548; V. The Thanksgiving is based on M. Rihel's chorale of 1570, *Wir danken deiner Wohltat gross.*

In the Creed Distler's use of a Bicinium for the section dealing with "the Son, our Lord Jesus Christ," points the way to his technique of ever more delicate and more intimate ensemble combinations. In the Words of Institution, his variation of Luther's *formulae,* consisting mainly of filling in melodic leaps, makes an interesting study:

Ex. 56. The *Vox Evangelista:*[2]

Ex. 57. The *Vox Christi:*

Ex. 58.

Ex. 59.

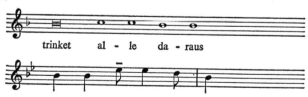

Ex. 60.

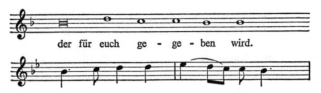

der für euch ge - ge - ben wird.

Ex. 61.

so oft ihr's tut zu mei-nem Ge-dächt-nis.
(trin-ket)

These Words of Institution from Luther's Mass are sung by a solo soprano, while a small group sings the chorale as an accompaniment.

The Thanksgiving features alternations between the whole choir and a smaller group, as well as some fine writing for various combinations of voices: the two soprano parts alone; the three lower voices without the second bass; the three upper parts (two sopranos and alto). Text painting for the first basses to the words ("and never an end . . .") outlines the minor seventh, a favorite Distler interval:

Ex. 62. P. 21, Mm. 5 14.

da nim-mer, da nim - mer ein En — — —

— de, ein En — — — —

A 2-page Amen of seraphic beauty brings to a close Distler's opus 3.

Although Distler chose to title this composition "Little Advent Music," it is small neither in concept nor in message. Perhaps it is "little" regarding the modest forces it employs: a 3-part choir (soprano, alto, baritone); solo instruments: flute, oboe, violin, and organ (or harpsichord or piano); and optional parts for cello and narrator. In concept and length, however, the "Little Advent Music" is Distler's largest cantata for voices and instruments.

It is based on the Advent chorale *Nun komm, der Heiden Heiland,* a germanization of St. Ambrose's hymn *Veni, Redemptor gentium.* Luther is credited with the German text, which, along with its pre-Reformation tune, appeared in the Wittenberg *Geistliches Gesang-büchlein* of 1524.

The composition presents a well-conceived, symmetrical formal plan, an arch with a keystone, not unlike that of a Bach cantata such as No. 4, *Christ lag in Todesbanden.*

Sonata (instruments alone)
Stanza 1 (choir and instruments)
Stanza 2 (choir, oboe, violin, and organ)
Stanza 3 (sopranos; interludes for instruments alone)
Stanza 4 (prelude and postlude for organ alone; choir a cappella)
Stanza 5 (instrumental fugue; bass solo)
Stanza 6 (soprano and alto duet, obbligato instruments)
Stanza 7 (choir and instruments)
Sonata (instruments alone)

The instrumental Sonata that frames the work is in ABA form, with the cantus firmus played throughout by the flute. One spot illustrating particular rhythmic complexity is the measure immediately preceding the return of *A,* measure 23.[3]

The opening chorale setting of *Nun komm, der Heiden Heiland* used by Distler was also published in his *Der Jahrkreis* opus 5. In the cantata the cantus is heard in an unornamented version played by the oboe. A most interesting texture is achieved by the use of three obbligato instruments, all of which play in approximately the same range. In the vocal parts this stanza is primarily a straightforward setting of the chorale, with some rhythmic variation in the alto part.

Following this introductory chorale stanza is section one, "The Promise." The narrator tells of John the Baptist, forerunner of Christ, and the choir responds with the second stanza of the chorale. In this setting the organ assumes an obbligato function, its part being designed to be played at 4-foot pitch throughout. Above the imitative choral parts, the two obbligato instruments, oboe and violin, weave a delicate instrumental tracery.

Part two, "The Annunciation," begins with the passage from St. Luke that tells of the angel Gabriel's visit to the Virgin Mary. An instrumental ritornello, played by the flute, oboe, and violin, introduces the melismatic setting of the chorale's third stanza for sopranos and organ; this ritornello, heard five times, separates the four lines of the text. The choral writing here is an early example of unbarred music in Distler's catalog.

Section three, "The Visit to Elizabeth," is introduced by further Gospel passages from St. Luke; an a cappella chorale harmonization of stanza four is framed by an organ chorale prelude, heard both before and after the chorale.

Part four, "Mary's Song of Praise" (Magnificat), is an instrumental fugue of great rhythmic vitality, to which is added the fifth stanza of the chorale as a bass solo. The second section of the instrumental accompaniment is in gigue rhythm, with effective use of the organ in response to the other instruments.

Part five, "The Journey to Bethlehem," is introduced by the familiar words, "In those days a decree went out from Caesar Augustus," and is, musically, the most tender of the cantata's settings. The sopranos and altos sing the sixth stanza of the chorale with a gentle flute accompaniment, largely in triplets; the organ, oboe, and violin respond with the chorale as an echo to each phrase sung (the chorale proper is in the violin part). All the parts are heard simultaneously for the final phrase.

Part six, "The Fulfillment," begins with John 1:14-16, "And the Word became flesh and dwelt among us," followed by a repetition of the opening chorale harmonization to the Gloria Patri text, "Praise to God the Father be . . ." The repetition of the opening Sonata closes the form and brings to a conclusion a veritable sermon in Scripture and music.

The first performance of this work in 1931, on the first Sunday in Advent, was done with harpsichord and cello instead of organ. Breitkopf and Härtel published the score in 1932, the last of Distler's works to appear from this publisher.

Der Jahrkreis, opus 5

Dedicated to Pastor Axel Werner Kühl as a "continuing remembrance of our work together," *Der Jahrkreis* (The Year's Cycle) consists of 52 three-part chorale settings. Most of these were sung by Distler's children's choir at St. Jakobi; in those which have baritone parts, Distler himself sang this lower part while the children sang the upper two. These settings illustrate most ably what can be done for church music with limited means.

In a letter to Hermann Grabner dated April 17, 1931, only 4½ months after he began his duties at St. Jakobi, Distler wrote,

> I have two choirs (a volunteer church choir and a boy choir) for which I compose everything myself. I already have a beautiful collection of this type of easy sacred music and hope that an entire year's repertoire will come into being from this. The children as well as the adults sing these easy polyphonic pieces with joy and ease.

The melodies used for these 52 compositions Ursula von Rauchhaupt tabulated as follows:

Of 43 chorales, 34 melodies (33 texts) stem from the period of the Reformation; 8 melodies (10 texts) are from the time of Paul Gerhardt (the 17th century). Only one, *Macht hoch die Tür,* No. 6, is from a later time — and it is not much later. The melody is from Halle, 1704; the text, by Georg Weissel, is from 1642.[4]

Thus it may easily be figured that 79 percent of the melodies used are Reformation era melodies, leaving 21 percent as 17th-century tunes. Of the nine compositions which are not based on chorales, the following disposition may be made:

Two are folksongs — *Maria durch ein' Dornwald ging* and *Wohlauf mit mir auf diesen Plan.*

Five are Scriptural motets — from the Psalms, *Gott ist unsere Zuversicht* and *Wie der Hirsch schreiet;* from the Gospels, *Also hat Gott die Welt geliebet* and *Ein neu Gebot gebe ich euch;* and from the Apocalypse, *Selig sind die Toten.*

One composition is to a text by Mörike, foreshadowing the great cycle of the *Mörike-Chorliederbuch,* opus 19: *Herr schicke, was du willst.*

And the final number, 52, is comprised of three settings of the word "Amen."

As regards musical forces employed in these settings:

Eleven feature a change between Tricinia and Bicinia.

One has the contrast of a single-line melody with the Tricinium.

Three are provided with instrumental ritornelli in the style of the *Glogauer* and *Lochamer Liederbücher.*

The very first composition, *O Heiland, reiss die Himmel auf,* shows the first example in Distler's works of the simultaneous use of varying time signatures:

Ex. 63. P. 4, Score 1.

Although there are many meter changes in the succeeding compositions, this free barring in the individual parts is used at only two other places in *Der Jahrkreis:* at No. 10 and in the second stanza (Bicinium) of No. 33.

114

A few of the settings in opus 5 reappear at other spots in
Distler's printed works: No. 3 and No. 8, settings of *Nun komm,
der Heiden Heiland,* are the settings already used in the *Kleine Adventsmusik,* opus 4. No. 47, *Christ, der du bist der helle Tag,* will
be seen again as the chorale harmonization of the *Kleine geistliche
Abendmusik,* opus 6/I; and a more concealed borrowing is that of
No. 14, *Jesu, deine Passion,* which appears, transposed one step
higher, as the second stanza of the *Choralpassion,* opus 7.

Distler's searching for various means to conquer the tyranny of
the barline is expressed in yet another way in No. 16, *Also hat
Gott die Welt geliebet.* He uses eighth notes barred across a measure
as well as two asymmetric meter signatures in this short example:

Ex. 64. P. 28, Mm. 1-7.

In one of the loveliest of the *Jahrkreis* compositions, No. 35,
Selig sind die Toten, the first part is scored without barlines at all;
with its alternation between soloist and chantlike lower parts, this
selection achieves a special feeling of rhythmic freedom, as well as
a deeply peaceful mood, expressive of the text, "Blessed are the
dead who die in the Lord."

Ex. 65. P. 63, Score 1.

No. 33, *Est ist das Heil uns kommen her,* offers an early example of a "Distler melisma" in the soprano, as well as some interesting meter changes in the lines following:

Ex. 66. P. 58, Mm. 4-5.

Ex. 67. P. 58, Mm. 9-11.

In fact, *Der Jahrkreis* might be considered a sort of primer to Distler's ideas concerning text setting, melodic construction, and rhythmic subleties, much as Bach's *Orgelbüchlein* shows, in miniature, nearly every facet of his genius with the organ chorale prelude. Distler's *Jahrkreis* remains ideal music to fulfill the function for which it was written: contemporary church music that is usable in almost any situation, and music for the quality of which no apologies need to be made. Some of the composer's most appealing choral works are found in these pages.

Christ, der du bist der helle Tag, opus 6/I

The *Kleine geistliche Abendmusik* is in the form of a short Rondocantata (ABACA). It is scored very simply for 3-part choir (soprano, alto, men's voices), organ, and two obbligato instruments, which may be two violins, two oboes or other woodwinds, or a mixture of these. The chorale on which the cantata is based was not found in the Lübeck *Gesangbuch* of 1931, the chorale book in use at St. Jakobi. Distler's source was probably the *Berneuchener Kreis Geistliche Abendlieder,* published by the Bärenreiter-Verlag in 1930.

The work opens without introduction with the chorale's first stanza, *Christ, der du bist der helle Tag:*

Ex. 68. P. 3, Mm. 1-3.

It is this harmonization of the chorale, accompanied by organ and both obbligato instruments, which is repeated to a new stanza text to form the recurring part of the rondo form.

The second section utilizes the text from St. Luke 24, "Lord, remain with us, for it is near evening and the day is departing." This stanza is characterized by alternation of the voices and obbligato instruments. At the final cadence of this section the instruments have a duet in open fifths above the final sustained chord of the choir; the instruments, cadencing on *E* and *B,* transform the final chord into a seventh chord on *C,* the dominant as far as the tonality of the entire cantata is concerned:

Ex. 69. P. 8, Mm. 1-5.

Following the second stanza of the opening chorale, section
four of the cantata, for a solo soprano, begins with five measures
for the obbligato instruments without organ continuo. The soprano
and organ then enter to proclaim the words of Psalm 91: "The
Lord is thy Shield." To conclude this section the choir repeats the

motive sung by the soprano, but with a change in text to "The Lord is *my* Shield, I will trust in my God."

The concluding stanza of the chorale breathes a benediction to all who sing or hear it:

> So sleep we now in Thy dear name,
> Safe while Thy angel doth remain.
> Thou holy, blessed Trinity,
> We praise Thee now, eternally.

Drei kleine Choralmotetten, opus 6/II

These three motets are among the most popular of Distler's compositions. Published individually and within the capabilities of most choirs, they are excellent examples of truly practical and artistic *Gebrauchsmusik* for the contemporary church.

Number one, *Es ist das Heil uns kommen her,* consists of three stanzas, the second of which is a Bicinium. The chorale melody in the soprano is parodied immediately by the vigorous ascending bass line:

Ex. 70. P. 1, Score 1.

A contemporary use of hocket may be seen on the first page of this motet:

Ex. 71. P. 1, Score 3.

Following the Bicinium, in which the cantus firmus remains in the soprano while the alto sings a second part, the third stanza begins with an E-flat triad motive echoed back and forth between the upper two and the lower two voices. With the petition "And deliver us from evil," sung very peacefully, and a broadening final "Amen," this first small motet is brought to a conclusion.

Number two, *Komm, heiliger Geist, Herre Gott,* is a 2-stanza setting of the Pentecost hymn. Fourths and fifths predominate in the harmonic material; unbarred, the work progresses solidly to its forte *Hallelujah* ending.

Number three, *Lobe den Herren, den mächtigen König der Ehren!* is the most popular of the three. Very traditional in its construction, using barlines to separate its changing meters, Distler himself often wondered if this motet were not too close to the style of the old masters. At the cadences, however, his soaring melismas, a 7/4 meter, or the insistent repetition of a motive stamps it unmistakably as Distler rather than some earlier composer. For this motet, which has sold hundreds of thousands of copies in Germany alone, the composer received a payment of 10 marks!

The first stanza, in four parts, is followed by a Tricinium and a repetition of the opening stanza. The well-known Joachim Neander chorale is easily heard throughout this motet. The concluding four measures of each stanza will serve as examples of the spirit and compositional techniques pervading this lively motet:

Ex. 72. P. 2, Mm. 2-5.

Ex. 73. P. 2. (Stanza 2), Mm. 19-23.

Choralpassion, opus 7

Distler stated in the postscript *(Nachwort)* to his *Choralpassion* that he had been moved to compose this work through the impressions made on him by the yearly performance of the Schütz *St. Matthew Passion,* which Grusnick had made traditional at St. Jakobi in Lübeck. Because of his admitted debt to the pre-Bach master, a comparison of Distler's *Passion* to Schütz works in this genre may be both instructive and enlightening. Dorothee Stein has made some comparisons that may be of use:

1. Distler displays a stronger sense of form, possibly because, after the 19th-century triumph of the symphonic poem, form in the new music, and especially in the new church music, had a special meaning and symbolic power.

2. This thought-out form is apparent in the composition of the choruses; while Schütz through-composed the text (with one exception, *Ja nicht auf das Fest* from the *Matthäus-Passion*), Distler customarily repeated the first lines of the texts to make a closed 3-section form.

3. The recitatives of both masters are similar in form. Distler's, not so much influenced by the Italian opera, are actually more archaic in flavor than those of Schütz! The use of barlines in Distler's *Passion* makes really no difference, for both composers followed speech rhythm.

4. Distler's choruses are at least as dramatic as those of

121

Schütz, and perhaps even more so, for he uses rhythmic crescendi to achieve great excitement, a mirror of our time.

5. Distler framed his work and separated its sections by using a chorale; here he was closer to Bach than to Schütz.

6. For both, church music was closely bound up with liturgy.[5]

A further similarity to Schütz may be noticed in Distler's formal plan for the *Passion*. While Distler utilizes the entire passion story from all four gospels, a "Passion-Harmony," his formal scheme follows closely that used by Schütz in the *Lukas-Passion*. Each divides the work into seven sections:

Schütz	*Distler*
Eingang	
I. Judas — Hohepriester Rat	I. Einzug (Palm Sunday)
II. Abendmahl	II. Judas — Pharisäer Rat
III. Gethsemane	III. Abendmahl
IV. Petrus und Kaiphas	IV. Der Garten
V. Pilatus	V. Kaiphas
VI. Golgatha	VI. Pilatus
VII. Grablegung	VII. Golgatha
Beschluss	Final Chorale

Distler's work is highly individual, however, in its firm basis on one chorale melody; indeed the *Passion* is a "chorale partita" based on *Jesu, deine Passion,* with the drama of the story enacted between the stanzas of the chorale. With eight stanzas of the chorale, 20 *turba* choruses, and the recitatives Distler tells the Passion history.

New, also, in his work is a rudimentary motive symbolism, bound up with text painting. A particular example of the expressive possibility this technique affords is the diminished fifth on the word *Tode:*

Ex. 74. P. 18, Part IV, Score 6.

Evangelist

und es kam, dass er mit dem To - de rang,

which is echoed one page later when the mob seizes Jesus in the garden, the action which represents the first community step toward His death:

Ex 75. P. 19, Score 5.

Evangelist

und sie leg - ten ih - re Hän - de an Je - sum,

Again this same diminished fifth characterizes Jesus' words "You have spoken it," which leads the mob to scream, "He hath blasphemed God," a further step on the way to the cross:

Ex. 76. P. 23, Score 7.

Jesus

" Ihr sa - get es."

The final commentary on the dying Savior, sung by the Evangelist, "And He bowed His head and died," utilizes the augmented fourth — another reference to the symbolic interval in inversion?

Ex. 77. P. 51, Score 11.

Evangelist

und nei - get sein Haupt und ver - schied.

Several further examples of text painting in the recitatives deserve special mention. The opening note of the Evangelist is a whole-note on *C,* and the word is, fittingly enough, *Viel* — "many." The chromatic melisma in a minor tonality illustrates the word of Jesus, *leide* — "suffer."

Ex. 78. P. 15, Score 7.

Jesus

eh dass ich lei – – – – de. Wahr-lich,

The word following the melisma, *Wahrlich* ("truly"), uses the perfect fourth, an interval which seems to be used often in the recitatives of Jesus to characterize the purity and forcefulness of the Savior.

Chromaticism is used in various places throughout the *Choralpassion* more as a melodic than a harmonic device. It expresses the uncertainty of the questioning disciples when, with their troubled "Lord, is it I?" they respond to the Lord's statement that someone is to betray Him. A descending chromatic scale is the motive that portrays the shiftiness of the hypocritical crowd in the *turba* chorus *Wir haben keinen König* ("We have no king but Caesar").

Distler's choruses, set for 5-part choir (two soprano parts), are marvels of dramatic portrayal. After the opening chorale stanza and the setting of the scene by the Evangelist, the first chorus is the Palm Sunday drama, "Hosanna to the one who comes in the name of the Lord." A striking commentary on the fickleness of the crowd and a superb formal sense are both evident in Distler's repetition of this opening chorus as the final *turba* chorus, to the text "He trusted in God, let God now deliver Him from the cross, if He be the king of Israel!"

The eight stanzas of the chorale *Jesus, deine Passion,* which serve as beginning, end, and division points throughout the *Passion,* are handled with so much variety that there is no chance for monotony. After the first stanza's quiet, full five parts, the second presents a harmonization for three women's voices; the third, to the text *O hilf, Christe* — the text of the final chorus of the Schütz *Johannes-Passion,* is again for five voices, but with a closing section in 6/4 meter to add variety.

The chorus of false witnesses in only two parts (alto and tenor) achieves variety and great rhythmic emphasis. Indeed, as usual, Distler's rhythm must be singled out as a most novel feature of his choral writing. The setting of the words *Wir dürfen niemand töten* with its two sixteenth notes on the single syllable *Wir* is striking and impelling in its rough forcefulness:

Ex. 79. P. 33, Mm. 1-3.

The use of a soprano melisma in the chorus "Crucify him" is both effective and original:

Ex. 80. P. 38, Mm. 1-6.

For the most part Distler remained within the bounds of traditional notation practices for this work: that is, most of the choruses are given meter signatures and barlines. Chorus No. 10, however, has two simultaneous meters: 3/4 in the upper three voices, 4/4 in the lower two, and some of the choral sections are unbarred. Thus in his notational techniques he was moving toward the next step, which was to be the separate barring of the individual parts, as seen in the *Weihnachtsgeschichte,* opus 10. The fact that Distler could offer so much vitality of rhythm and so much that was new within more traditional bounds probably accounts for the remarkable success of the *Choralpassion:* at least 17 major performances in Germany in the first year after it was published. Its popularity has remained undiminished; a note in the 1949 reprint of the work announced that it was being reoffered after the destruction of the plates during the war through a "gift of the Swedish Church as an aid project to the Evangelical Church of Germany." Thus, one of Distler's first works to be available again after the war, it has continued to bring its dramatic setting of our Lord's pain and death to the Christians of today.

The comparison of Distler with Schütz remains fascinating in biographical details as well as musical ones. Schütz took his position at the Dresden *Hofkapelle* one year before the outbreak of the Thirty Years' War; Distler lived in a period of two world wars. Both lived at the ends of certain periods of national culture. As with artistic men always, each felt the breakdown of his own world more deeply than those around him, and this deep impression shows through in the longing for death apparent in each man's work: Schütz at 40 (1625) wrote his *De vitae fugacitate* (Aria à 5), 11 years later his *Requiem.* Distler at 24 wrote the *Passion;* two years later followed the *Totentanz* motet and the motet *Ich wollt, dass ich daheime wär.* "Both saw that through their music they must be preachers of the Word, to proclaim in a proper sense the Gospel, healing power of the life, death, and resurrection of our Lord."[6]

Die Weihnachtsgeschichte, opus 10

A companion piece to the *Choralpassion,* the "Christmas Story" is set for 4-part chamber choir and four soloists (Evangelist, Angel, Mary, and Herod). This work, too, is in the form of a chorale partita, the seven stanzas of the chorale *Es ist ein Ros' entsprungen* forming the connecting links between the narration of the Christmas Gospel. In addition, the whole is framed with two large Scriptural motets, "The people who wandered in darkness" (Is. 9:2) at the beginning and "For God so loved the world" (John 3:16) at the conclusion.

In this work Distler forsook the regular barline as a notational device and barred each part in its individual rhythm; in addition to this way of writing the choral parts, the soloists' parts are notated in blackened note heads without stems, to insure that the parts will be sung in speech rhythm. The result of these unconventionalities in notation, after the initial problems of ensemble have been overcome, is a rare freedom from "rhythmic thump" and regularly recurring accent.

As an example of the variety desired in the performance of the freely notated recitatives, Distler has placed a rhythmically notated version below the song of Mary (the Magnificat), which is chanted above the third stanza of the chorale. This Magnificat is in the ninth tone of the German office psalmody, a modified *tonus peregrinus.*[7]

Ex. 81. P. 13, Score 7; P. 14, Score 1.

The rhythmical subtlety of Distler's text setting is evident throughout this work. One exceptional example, still in the metrical score of the Magnificat, is this spot with its double measure signature:

Ex. 82. P. 14, Score 2.

denn er hat die   Nie-drig-keit sei-ner   Magd

Here he uses both meter signatures because the quarter notes on *sein-* must not sound like a syncopation in 3/4 meter, but rather as the less accented fourth and fifth beats of a 6/8 measure.

The recitatives in *Die Weihnachtsgeschichte* have an even more archaic flavor than those of the *Choralpassion*. This is due largely to the highly pentatonic character of these later compositions. Two examples are quoted from the opening recitative of the Evangelist:

Ex. 83. P. 11, Score 2.

die heisst Na – – za – reth,

Ex. 84. P. 11, Score 3.

und die Jung – frau hiess Ma-ri – – a.

Distler's powers of text painting through music are again much in evidence in the opening chorus of *Die Weihnachtsgeschichte*. Especially lovely is the sudden hush at the words "and He shall be called 'Wonderful' " and the prolongation of the figure for the words "Eternal Father."

Ex. 85. P. 6, Score 4.

A favorite device of the composer is heard again at his treatment of the text "And of peace [there shall be] no ending" — a device in which he moves the three upper voices in parallel motion against the lowest voice in contrary motion:

Ex. 86. P. 8, Mm. 1-5.

The treatment of the chorale stanzas is, once again, varied with great imagination. Particularly noteworthy are the combination of the third stanza with the Magnificat for solo soprano, already mentioned; the fourth stanza, with its rocking cradle song in the bass voices, divided into three parts;

Ex. 87. P. 16, Score 9.

and the double-chorus setting of stanza five.

The closing chorale stanza is, musically, a repetition of the open-ing harmonization. Following the closing motet, *Also hat Gott die Welt geliebet,* is a characteristically beautiful extended "Amen."

In the new edition of this work in 1948 Bruno Grusnick indicated several deletions that Distler had discussed, authorized in rehearsals, or planned to make for a new edition. Unfortunately this projected revised edition was never realized by the composer himself, and the present-day performer is faced with the difficult choice of follow-ing the printed text or of accepting Grusnick's changes. Either way this work remains one of Distler's most charming, tender, and intimate, ideally suited to the Christmas season.

Wo Gott zum Haus nit gibt sein Gunst, opus 11/I
Nun danket all und bringet Ehr, opus 11/II

Two chorale cantatas make up the contents of opus 11. Interest-ing parallels with previous works appear in both compositions: the first is quite similar in form to the *Kleine Adventsmusik;* the second, to the *Kleine geistliche Abendmusik.* Distler remarks in his preface to the first of these two cantatas that they are attempts, even as the previous two compositions were, to provide *Gebrauchsmusik* for the worship service, music of limited technical difficulty to include many types of instruments. In the spirit of *Gebrauchsmusik,* Distler again makes provision for various combinations of instruments, and for the use of any one of three keyboard instruments: harpsichord, organ, or piano.

The instrumentation for the cantata *Wo Gott zum Haus* includes two oboes, a string quartet (which may be expanded in numbers), and a keyboard instrument. The work opens with a sinfonia: three measures of andante introduction followed by a chorale prelude in which the strings and keyboard treat the chorale in fugato while the two oboes have a slightly ornamented version of the melody.

The opening chorale stanza employs the strings to double the choral parts while the oboes have a jolly obbligato.

Ex. 88. P. 7, Chorale, Mm. 1-3.

The second stanza, set for soprano and alto duet (which may be sung by soloists or by the respective sections of the choir), is accompanied by the strings and keyboard instrument. The second section of this stanza, marked "molto tranquillo" employs the keyboard instrument playing at 4-foot pitch (one octave higher than written for the piano), the vocal parts in dotted whole notes (in 6/4 meter), and muted strings to portray the gift of sleep *(gibt er's im Schlaf)*.

The chorale is repeated to stanza three, the musical setting being the same. Then follows the fourth stanza as a duet for tenor and bass with an accompaniment very reminiscent of baroque practice: the keyboard and cello playing in octaves throughout.

The Sinfonia is repeated, followed by the fifth stanza of the chorale, a Gloria Patri. Ending the work with the chorale stanza rather than with the Sinfonia makes an interesting change in the form, rather an arch with one misplaced pillar!

Nun danket all is even shorter and simpler, very much the rondo form so loved by the composer. The instrumentation for this work dispenses with winds, and utilizes four strings (with an optional contrabass) and organ. The first, third, and fifth stanzas of the chorale, all set to the same music, are printed in hymnbook fashion, one under the other. After a brief, 2-page prelude, the first stanza is sung. The second stanza, for soprano solo, is accompanied by the organ, the first violin, and the cello, which serves the function here of a basso continuo instrument.

After the third stanza of the chorale, the fourth is set most simply for tenor solo, an unornamented setting of the chorale, accompanied throughout in octaves by the strings and keyboard.

The most elaborate of the stanzas is the sixth, set for soprano and tenor duet, with some concertante writing for the strings. The prelude and first stanza are repeated to conclude this cantata.

Geistliche Chormusik, opus 12

The nine motets which comprise opus 12 are the crowning achievements of Distler's sacred choral music. This series, originally planned to include an anthem for each Sunday of the liturgical year, was unfortunately never completed. The first seven motets date from the years 1934 to 1937; the final two are from the Berlin years.

No. 1, *Singet dem Herrn ein neues Lied* (O Sing to the Lord a New Song), is a motet for Cantate, the Fourth Sunday After Easter. The vigorous opening motive, sung in octaves by the men, gives evidence that it will indeed be a "new song":

Ex. 89. P. 5, Mm. 1-4.

The sopranos and altos begin a dotted motive:

Ex. 90. P. 5, Mm. 4-5.

This leads to a repetition of the opening phrase, one tone higher; then another repetition, yet another tone higher; while the lower voices proclaim, "for He doeth wondrous things," and the sopranos sustain an 8-measure inverted pedal point on *E*.

The second section of the motet begins with the rhythmic presentation of the text *Und er sieget mit seiner Rechten,* above which a melody is developed in the soprano.

Ex. 91. P. 6, Mm. 1-3.

The second section contains a development of the motive presented in the first part for the word *Singet.* An ecstatic melisma in parallel fifths between soprano and alto above the men's voices singing repeatedly the words *lobet, singet* closes this second section.

Part three begins with the favorite Distler device, pairs of parallel voices in contrary motion to each other:

Ex. 92. P. 12, Mm. 1-3.

At the text *und mit Trompeten* a technique reminiscent of the double notes to a single syllable of the *Wir dürfen niemand töten* from the *Choralpassion* is heard:

Ex. 93. P. 12, M. 14.

This use of double notes for a single syllable provides an exciting roughness of rhythm and a color both unusual and fitting for this text.

At the words "and be joyful" the upper three voices move in parallel motion in a melisma, while the basses sustain an E pedal point. In a footnote the composer has defended himself from the accusation that he might be "atonally" minded with his E-sharp against the bass E-natural, explaining that the voice leading in the soprano requires the alteration.

Ex. 94. P. 14, Mm. 9-11.

With a repetition of the opening *Singet* motives, and another melisma in parallel fifths, nearly like the one which closed part two of this same motet, the work is concluded.

No. 2 is the *Totentanz* (Dance of Death), a motet for "Totensonntag," the Last Sunday After Trinity. This work is more fitting for a vesper service on this commemorative day than for a church worship service, for it utilizes not only a choir, but speakers as well. Fourteen choral settings based on texts extracted from *Der Cherubinische Wandersmann* of Angelus Silesius (Johannes Scheffler, 1624 to 1677) are interspersed by a re-creation of the medieval *Totentanz* texts from Lübeck's Marienkirche, arranged by the Lübeck poet Johannes Klöcking. In these dialogs Death speaks successively to Emperor, Bishop, Nobleman, Physician, Merchant, Knight, Sailor, Hermit, Peasant, Virgin, Old Man, and Tiny Child, inviting or commanding each to come to the final dance with him.

With such dramatic forces, Distler has achieved in this motet a work of great seriousness; it marks, in addition, the first of the opus 12 works to deal with an eschatological subject, indicative of his preoccupation with the life to come. No fewer than five more of the nine motets comprising the *Geistliche Chormusik* deal with, or suggest, the longing for life eternal.

Musically this work shows, in general, a more homophonic Distler than the other motets. Such passages as the beginning of the second section are quite typical of this work; here, reminiscent of the parallel organus of the Ars Antiqua, the voices will be found to move in octaves and fifths:

Ex. 95. P. 7, Mm. 6-10.

Homophonic texture is further apparent in such a passage as the 13th chorus, where the upper three voices move in parallel rhythms above a sustained pedal point:

Ex. 96. P. 20, Mm. 6-8.

Examples of various kinds of text painting are in evidence on every page of the *Totentanz*. A particularly effective one is found at the conclusion of the opening chorus, where the sopranos sing the words "In heaven is the day" and the basses respond, "Beneath, the earth is the night," to be answered by the two inner voices, "Here is the twilight."

Ex. 97. P. 6, Mm. 8-10; P. 7, Mm. 1-2.

The 11th chorus, representing the words which are addressed to the young Virgin, makes use of the motive of the upward perfect fifth to illustrate the words, *Auf, auf!* This is the signal motive of Distler's organ partita on *Wachet auf, ruft uns die Stimme* as well as of his motet on the same chorale.

The 14th and final chorus is a motet in itself, three pages in length, in ABA form, the first section a setting of the text "The soul born for eternity has no true rest in things of the present time." The "B" section very beautifully develops the motive set to the words *Keine wahre Ruh.*

Ex. 98. P. 21, Mm. 10-11.

A very shortened version of "A" is followed by a long coda, which concludes the motet with only a single line for the sopranos.

Wach auf, du deutsches Reich, No. 3, is for the festival of Reformation. This work is dwarfed by its surrounding companion pieces in the series, and is the weakest work of the nine. In rondo form, with the opening harmonization of the chorale serving quadruple duty as stanzas one, three, five, and seven of the motet, the work is rounded out by the intervening stanzas set respectively for four parts, four choral parts with two soprano solo parts (ending with six chorus parts), and again four parts, dominated by the motive "Wach auf!" In the rondo stanzas, the chorale is heard in the bass, with some canonic imitation in the soprano.

Of far greater charm and compositional mastery is No. 4, a motet for Christmas, *Singet frisch und wohlgemut.* This motet, in three sections, uses the German folk tune *Joseph, lieber Joseph mein.* The cradle song character of the tune is emphasized by the refrain *Eia* ("Lullay") above the tune, which is sung in a low register by the basses. This use of the full range of all voices is another typical feature of Distler's vocal style.

Ex. 99. P. 4, Mm. 2-7.

In contrast to this gently moving cradle song comes the following section in which each voice proclaims in turn "Today is born the Lord Christ," to which the entire choir responds, "Emmanuel." With two lovely melismas on the word "Emmanuel" in the soprano, the first section of the motet is brought to a close.

The second section of *Singet frisch und wohlgemut* is, typically for Distler, a Bicinium for soprano and alto. The composer's mastery is never more in evidence than in these spots where he is working with reduced forces, and this gentle stanza is no exception.

The third stanza, a very peaceful and quietly moving homophonic setting of the chorale, concludes richly with six parts, provided by divided alto and bass parts. Above the tonic and dominant pedals in the bass, the soprano sings an evocative melisma on the word *Ewigkeit* ("eternity").

Ex. 100. P. 12, Mm. 12-16.

No. 5 is a setting of Laufenberg's chorale text *Ich wollt dass ich daheime wär*. For sheer beauty of text setting and sensuousness of sound, these five pages are not surpassed in Distler's choral writing. The first chorale phrase is heard at the beginning of the motet in the soprano:

Ex. 101. P. 3, Mm. 1-5.

Distler's variation technique is illustrated by the various lines he combines with this melody at succeeding stages of the motet. Immediately following the soprano statement quoted above, the altos sing the melody, above which the sopranos have a melismatic line with the triplets so often associated with the word "heaven" in Distler's works.

Ex. 102. P. 3, Mm. 6-7.

Further on in the motet comes an even more melismatic line for the sopranos above the chorale in the tenor part:

Ex. 103. P. 6, Mm. 5-7.

The conclusion of this motet breathes a hopefulness and calmness before death, perhaps even a longing for death, which is the essence of true Christian belief in the superiority of the hereafter to life on earth. The text reads, "Farewell, world, and be blessed! I journey now to the heavenly kingdom," and Distler's setting of this text, heightened by a gentle uncertainty of mode (a chromatic change between F-sharp and F-natural suggests first Ionian or major, then Mixolydian), ends rather quietly but also triumphantly with an E-major chord.

No. 6 is another composition for the Last Sunday After Trinity, the motet on the chorale *Wachet auf, ruft uns die Stimme*. This motet is the only one in the *Geistliche Chormusik* which is set for five voices.

The ascending figure to the text *Wachet auf*, the "signal" motive, dominates the opening page, introduced first in each voice, and then combined with other voices to make a vocal fanfare. The cantus firmus appears in the lowest of the five parts. For the repeated opening phrase of the chorale, the melody appears in the tenor, then returns to the bass.

The use of double inflections between parts creates some interesting chromaticism for the text "[Midnight] calls us with bright mouth . . .":

Ex. 104. P. 6, Mm. 13-14.

Shortly after these full and chromatic sounds Distler reduces his forces to only two parts in octaves, an effective contrast. This same figure, immediately raised a minor third, heightens the text, *Wohlauf!*

Ex. 105. P. 7, Mm. 8-9.

Stanza two begins with two soprano voices singing the slightly ornamented cantus in canon. Beneath this duet the chorale is sung by the choir (still in five parts). This stanza ends with a contemplative "Hosanna." A melisma in parallel fourths for the two solo sopranos ends on F-sharp and B, above the choir's sustained C-major chord. This final chord with unresolved seventh recalls the instrumental obbligato from the second stanza of the cantata, opus 6/I, the *Kleine geistliche Abendmusik*.

Stanza three, also beginning with three measures of chorus soprano duet, has the cantus treated polyphonically in traditional motet style. Interesting cross accents between two pairs of voices occur in a 3/2 section to the text *Solche Freude* ("such joy"). With a single line to proclaim "Thus praise we and sing" and *divisi* in all parts except the alto and bass to make an 8-part final chord, the motet concludes in contrast and jubilance.

The work made a remarkable impression at its first hearing in Kassel in 1935, and its popularity remains great in present-day Germany. With the full sonorities, an impressionistic use of parallel fifths, sevenths, and occasional ninths, with rhythmic skill and intricacy, and with the vitality of the chorale itself to undergird the composition, this popularity is not difficult to comprehend.

In der Welt habt ihr Angst, No. 7, is the shortest motet of the nine. A setting of John 16:33, "In the world you have tribulation; but be of good cheer, I have overcome the world," it was composed in a few hours as a burial motet for the composer's mother-in-law, Frau Thienhaus. The setting of this text, so applicable to the composer himself, serves as an antiphon to the chorale *Wenn mein Stündlein vorhanden ist.*

Noteworthy in the setting of this text is the syncopation for the word *habt,* the chromatic inflections in the bass line to illustrate the word *Angst* ("anxiety" or "tribulation"), and the major mode feeling for the text *aber seid getrost* ("but be of good cheer").

Ex. 106. P. 2, M. 1.

Ex. 107. P. 2, Mm. 4-5.

The chorale setting is a straightforward one with the cantus firmus in the soprano throughout.

The final two motets of the *Geistliche Chormusik* represent Distler's last sacred compositions and date from his early days in Berlin. In a letter to his friend Ingvar Sahlin (to whom the Cantata, opus 11/I, is dedicated) in September 1941, Distler wrote, "Just now there are again newly in print several compositions which will be sure to interest you: two large new motets, *Fürwahr, er trug unsere Krankheit* and *Das ist je gewisslich wahr.*"

These two motets, originally planned as opening and closing motets for the never completed *St. John Passion,* are both united with chorale settings. No. 8, *Das ist je,* ends with the chorale *Ehre sei dir, Christe,* and No. 9, *Fürwahr, er trug,* concludes with *Ein Lämmlein geht und trägt die Schuld.*

These final two motets by Distler show clearly that his tonal ideal was expanding, and they heighten the impression that, had he lived longer, his art would not have remained a static thing. The chromaticism of motet nine, extreme for Distler, remained within tonal bounds and linear possibilities, but it could be regarded as an expansion from the composer's modal writing of the previous decade.

Das ist je gewisslich wahr is a setting of the text from 1 Tim. 1:15-16:

> The saying is sure and worthy of full acceptance, that Christ Jesus came into the world to save sinners. And I am the foremost of sinners; but I received mercy for this reason, that in me, as the foremost, Jesus Christ might display his perfect patience for an example to those who were to believe in him for eternal life. (RSV)

After 170 measures concerned with the setting of this text, there follows a section of 75 measures to the text *sei Ehre und Preis in Ewigkeit,* ("be honor and praise to eternity") — perhaps the length illustrative of the "eternity" mentioned in the text. A sequential treatment in which the two lower voices sing *sei Ehre und Preis* while the upper voices intone *in Ewigkeit* presents many interesting and effective cross accents.

The closing chorale ends with the petitions "Kyrie eleison, Christe eleison, Kyrie eleison" set in parallel octaves. Once again the utmost simplicity achieves the utmost in effectiveness. This motet would doubtless have been the concluding part of the projected *Passion.*

Even more exciting in conception, however, is the final motet, *Fürwahr, er trug unsere Krankheit.* The motive on which the motet is based is heard in the first two measures:

Ex. 108. P. 3, Mm. 1-2.

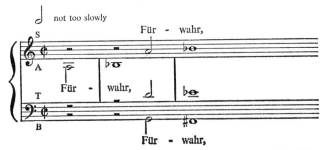

The text, Is. 53:4-5, "Surely he has borne our griefs," lends itself to this chromatic treatment. At the words "But he was wounded" a fugal section begins with this highly chromatic subject.

Ex. 109. P. 6, Mm. 11-19.

The cadence to this middle section is most effective. A feature of his choral style in general is his unashamed use of suspension figures and his ability to suggest true repose at cadential points.

Ex. 110. P. 9, Mm. 12-17.

The entire first section of the work (65 measures) is repeated. Some expressive dissonances are heard a few bars from the end:

Ex. 111. P. 5, Mm. 19-22.

The work is concluded with a simple harmonization of the chorale *Ein Lämmlein geht und trägt die Schuld*.

Thus we have come to the end of the survey of these nine motets in opus 12. Distler intended that this entire collection should be a continuation, or a repetition on a larger scale, of the church music for the liturgical year he had begun in *Der Jahrkreis*. From the intense jubilation of the first motet through the chromatic sadness of the last, the compositions not only express Christian truths but mirror the earthly fortunes of the composer as well. They are a legacy of great worth, representing Distler at his peak as a composer for the church.

Liturgische Sätze über altevangelische Kyrie- und Gloriaweisen, opus 13

Distler's opus 13 was published in 1936 and received immediate wide distribution throughout Germany, for it was sent to subscribers of the church music magazine *Musik und Kirche* as a companion piece to the sixth issue (November—December 1936). The collection consists of 28 settings of various melodies for the Lutheran Kyrie and Gloria in excelsis; the original melodies date from the years between 1525 and 1612.

Among the 28 settings, four are for two similar voices, one is for two dissimilar voices, three are for three similar voices, two are for 3-part choir, two are in three parts with solo parts in psalmodic style, ten are set for 4-part mixed chorus, two are for 4-part choir with soloists, four are set for 5-part mixed choir, and one is set for a 6-part choir. Various divided parts in these settings give as many as eight parts at times; in settings for double choruses the composer stipulates that the choruses shall be placed in different spots in the church.

From the tabulation of the various forces employed it may be seen that choirs of any size could use at least some of these settings, from the smallest parish church choir to the largest cathedral singing society. These compositions were intended as pure liturgical expressions, some of the first new liturgical music to come from the liturgical revival of the decade.

One of the most striking of these liturgical settings is the composition based on the *Nürnberger Grosses Gloria* of 1525, in a setting for solo soprano and 4-part mixed choir. The soloist sings the Gloria in the fourth tone, while the choir intones the first stanza of the German "Gloria," the chorale *Allein Gott in der Höh' sei Ehr.* Once again a comparison of the rhythmic setting which Distler has made with the melody as given in nonmetrical notation is most instructive concerning Distler's exactness and taste in setting the German language.

Ex. 112. P. 38, Mm. 2-6.

These settings obviously grew out of the inspiring liturgical setting of St. Jakobi in Lübeck, where it was possible to place the various choral groups in widely separated balconies, where the pastor was interested in a fresh and inspiring liturgical practice and was a fine enough musician himself to provide excellent intonations and chants in alternation from the altar, and where the ideal cooperation among choirmaster, organist, and clergy insured that such new settings as these could and would be used. The *Liturgische Sätze* are, then, *Gebrauchmusik* of a high order, worship music to enrich the contemporary church, pillars for the support of the liturgical renewal.

The works which have been noted and discussed in this chapter include the most important of Distler's sacred compositions. A number of chorale harmonizations and a few smaller motets were issued at various times by the Bärenreiter-Verlag as separate octavo issues. Among these are some excellent service music such as the motet *Ach Herr, ich bin nicht wert,* a setting of Matt. 8:8, noteworthy for its extended organum-like parallel fifths between alto and bass parts, a composition dated Sept. 5, 1937; the "Greeting-motet" for three equal voices, *Jesus Christus gestern und heute,* sent as a greeting to Dr. Otto Brodde of Dortmund, and featuring a flowing extended "Amen"; or the delicate setting of the Westphalian folksong for Christmas, *Su, su, su.* These add nothing different to the musical impressions made by the works with assigned opus numbers.

As has been repeatedly shown, Distler's art was definitely a vocal one; further, his life and work were inseparably bound up with the destiny of the church. He was more than a musician in his sacred music: he was a proclaimer of the Gospel, a tonal preacher. The tonal language he employed, the mixture of impressionism, archaic influences, the pentatonic scale, his predilection for pedal points, for rhythmic subdivision, for Baroque-flavored embellishment and ornamentation — all this combined gives his music something individual and recognizable. Distler remains Distler, and none of his contemporaries or successors has achieved the earnestness and ecstasy, the jubilation of his melismas and the spiritual depths of his text settings, or the idiomatic uses of the human voice that Distler achieved.

His work in church music, in the face of the severe Nazi opposition to such music, may be regarded as a resistance gesture. "Out of the situation of the Protestant church after 1933 the renewal of the polyphonic motet from the Reformation era has taken place as a true expression of the spirit of resistance," wrote Hans Mersmann in his introduction to the *Musica Nova* series of recordings.[8] "This, too, is far remote from the retreat into the historical — which is countered by the living power of the voice as part of the polyphonic tissue, by the intimate union of the artistic expression with religion."

The situation in Germany is no longer politically oppressive; the church is free to pursue its course again, and it now remains to be seen in this study whether or not the trends which started with Hugo Distler and his contemporaries are continuing in the new generation. What of his influence on those who have followed him?

NOTES TO CHAPTER 3

1. Oskar Söhngen, introduction to Cantate Record No. T72714 LP, "Geistliche Chormusik von Hugo Distler."
2. Examples 56–61 are from Ursula von Rauchhaupt, "Die vokale Kirchenmusik Hugo Distlers," p. 96 ff.; see also *Handbuch der deutschen evangelischen Kirchenmusik* (ed. Ameln, Mahrenholz), Vol. I, Part 1, pp. 296 and 315.
3. The complete score of this work, with an English text, is published by Concordia Publishing House, No. 97-6438.
4. Von Rauchhaupt, p. 27.
5. Freely adapted from Dorothee Stein, "Die Passionsgeschichte bei Heinrich Schütz und Hugo Distler" (unpublished dissertation, Kassel, n. d.), pp. 66–70; in the possession of the Hugo Distler-Archiv, Lübeck, Germany.
6. Freely translated from Stein, p. 2.
7. Von Rauchhaupt, p. 73.
8. Hans Mersmann, "Introduction" to *Musica Nova*, Series II (1958), published by the Deutsche Grammophon Gesellschaft (in Verbindung mit der deutschen Sektion des internationalen Musikrates), pp. 8 f.

CHAPTER 4

DISTLER'S INFLUENCE IN EUROPE AND AMERICA

"Influence," originally an astrological term meaning an ethereal fluid thought to flow from the stars and to affect the actions of men, is nearly as difficult to ascertain as if it were truly an emanation of occult power from the astral bodies! So much that molds and shapes the human mind is subconsciously assimilated that it becomes impossible to measure shaping forces and causes; in an art as subjective and indefinable as music this becomes especially true.

Distler, as a tragic figure, as the eternal seeker who died at an early age, has received much adulation from an ever growing circle in Germany. In the years since his untimely death the founding of Hugo Distler choirs and the organization of Distler festivals attests to his continuing and growing popularity. His music, thus often heard in performances, has already assumed a position as "classic" to the newer church music of Germany. Such festivals and tributes as the Berlin *Kirchenmusiktage* 1948, the 1952 celebrations in Kassel and Nuremberg (three concerts of Distler's works), and the *Distler-Gedenktage* in Hannover from November 8 through 11, 1958, in which Distler choirs of Berlin and Hannover took part, assure that Distler's music will be heard by many, including young composers and conductors.

As a choral conductor, Distler, himself very successful, inspired a whole generation of younger men, many of them active today as the leading choir trainers in Germany. Werner Berkenkamp, a talented young man who studied with Distler in Berlin, active in southern Germany; Gottfried Wolters, presently conductor of the *Norddeutscher Singkreis;* and Helmut Bornefeld — all well-known musicians today — were former students of Distler.

Distler's firm belief in the human voice as the ideal expressive medium, his novel and complex rhythmic demands on choirs, his utilization of the full range of the voices are all facets of his choral composition that have served as bases for the composers who have come after him.

Two men, in particular, will be considered here as direct Distler students: first, Jan Bender, one year younger than Distler, who studied with him at the Lübeck *Staatskonservatorium*. While the choral music of this composer, now a resident professor at Wittenberg University, Springfield, Ohio, often does not possess the rhythmic variety nor quite the impressionistic harmonic beauties of Distler's works, such a line as this from Bender's cantata *Now Let All Loudly Sing Praise to God,*[1] written in 1937, could scarcely be distinguished from a line of Distler's *Kleine geistliche Konzerte* for soprano and organ of the same period:

Ex. 113. Bender, *Cantata,* P. 14, Mm. 6-10

Even the optional use in this work of harpsichord or organ as keyboard continuo instrument is reminiscent of his teacher's practice.

In Bender's *The Sentences for the Seasons* (Concordia, 1959), he has, in best Distler tradition, placed the barlines between the staves rather than through them, a practice which stems, no doubt, from the transcription procedures of German musicologists of the early 20th century, and one adopted by Distler in his later works as another device in his unending battle against the barline.

One further example, this one from Bender's anthem *The Word Was Made Flesh* (Concordia, 1958), will suffice to show a possible Distler influence in his use of the soprano melisma to the text "The Word." The parallelism in the lower voices could also have come from a page of Distler's choral writing!

Ex. 114. Bender, *The Word Was Made Flesh*, P. 3, Mm. 1-3.

The second Distler pupil is Siegfried Reda, born in 1916, who studied with Pepping and Distler in Berlin. Especially in his organ works, Reda has carried on his own activity from the point where Distler's ceased. In his treatment of chorales, Reda seemed at first to be fulfilling Distler's desire for contemporary chorale harmonizations, somewhat in the manner of Distler's *Kleine Choralbearbeitungen,* opus 8/III. Such a work as Reda's *Choral- Spiel-Buch* for keyboard instruments (Bärenreiter Edition 2064, 1946), presents unbarred shorter chorale preludes for use on the organ, harpsichord, positiv, or harmonium.

In his volume entitled *Kleine Orgelstücke* (Bärenreiter Edition 1678, 1942), Reda has composed six small works for small instruments, much in the style of Distler's *Dreissig Spielstücke,* opus 18/I.

In later works for the organ, Reda has been experimenting with the possibilities of esoteric registrations, like Distler, composing "from" the organ as well as "for" it. The instrument presently at Reda's disposal in the Petrikirche in Mülheim an der Ruhr is a large contemporary instrument of four manual divisions built by Schuke.

The problem of the cantus firmus in organ composition is very much present in Reda's thinking and creative activity; he seems to be seeking a satisfactory solution for this difficult problem in such recent works as his Triptychon *O Welt, ich muss dich lassen* (1951) and his Meditation and Fugue *Wir danken dir, Herr Jesu Christ* (1960), in which he also employs voices. While he does not seem to have solved his formal problems as satisfactorily as had Distler, Reda's reliance, at least basically, on Baroque and pre-Baroque formal plans (concerti, chorale preludes, organ chorales, fugues, etc.) places him definitely in the line of succession from Pepping, David, and Distler as far as the annals of contemporary organ composition are concerned.

Even more recently in such a work as his Meditations on the Passion Chorale *Ein Lämmlein geht und trägt die Schuld,* Reda has devised a tone row by altering the lines of the chorale, and with this row he has fashioned a work in the tradition and techniques of Anton Webern. Reda feels strongly that unless the church can assimilate the techniques of the new music, it will be left hopelessly at the wayside in musical matters.[2]

Since Distler's music is relatively unknown in America, it is natural that his influence here should be less than in his native Germany. With such second generation composers as Bender now working in America, however, Distler's style and aesthetics of church music are bound to become better known among us.

Among younger American composers working in the sphere of church music, and in particular, church music for the Protestant liturgical service, one of the leading names is that of Richard Wienhorst (Ph. D., Eastman School of Music, 1961), professor of composition at Valparaiso University. Wienhorst knows the music of Distler from years of European study; such usages as his employment of unbarred, unaccompanied recitatives in note-head notation for the narrative parts of his *Nativity Cantata* (Summy, 1956), *The Seven Words from the Cross* (Concordia, 1956), and the Easter Cantata *Christ Jesus Lay in Death's Strong Bands* (Concordia, 1955), or the use of simultaneous 4/4 and 3/4 meters in his unison accompanied setting of "Behold, a Branch Is Growing" (from *Four Christmas Songs,* Concordia, 1960) — so reminiscent of Distler's treatment of this same chorale in *Die Weihnachtsgeschichte,* are visible reminders of the Distler legacy.

The spirit and liturgical framework in which Wienhorst composes, the first intangible, the latter clearly Lutheran, bring him again close to the young German master. Two quotations from Wienhorst's *Mass* in four parts (Associated Music Publishers, 1965) show a close affinity to Distler's melodic and harmonic practices:

Ex. 115. Wienhorst, *Mass,* P. 7, M. 1; P. 8, M. 1.

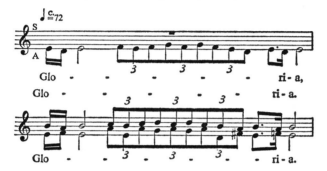

Ex. 116. Wienhorst, *Mass,* P. 30, Mm. 1-4.

In conversations with Wienhorst, as well as with Bender and musicians from several lands (Sweden, Denmark, Germany), the author has asked repeatedly whether or not the music of Distler has proved an inspiration or an influence in today's composition. The answer from all has been an emphatic Yes. As far back as 1937, Josef Hedar of Lund, Sweden, wrote that it would be to Germany that Swedish church musicians would have to look for inspiration to bring about the renewal of their own church music (see above, page 59). A recent visit to America by Harold Goransson, contemporary Swedish educator and church musician, gave us an opportunity to hear some of this new Scandinavian church music, indeed a vigorously flourishing school of choral composition.

Finally, the words with which Paul Collaer, a Belgian scholar, concludes his *History of Modern Music* concerning the position of the newer trends in 20th-century music as compared with that music of our century which is based on more traditional tonal resources seems to be both understanding and well expressed:

> . . . And yet we must not lose sight of the present cultural situation. Modern music that is truly representative of its time is not and cannot be the same in different parts of the world. Even within a single culturally homogeneous area, there will be different paths because many complexes of ideas and expression coexist. In Western Europe, for example, there are at present two distinct cultural currents.
>
> One of these currents follows the values that have been the basis of society for the last seven or eight thousand years: the values of agricultural peoples, whose musicians and poets even today sing of roses, nightingales, spring, and summer. . . .
>
> The other current, of recent origin, represents the urban and industrial culture which is still in the process of forming. For city people, who know nothing of the country except what they read in books, whistles and automobile horns replace the murmur of the woods and the water. A curve to them is an asphalt road; their rhythms translate rows of mercury lamps and the flickering of neon lights. Their sense of time does not reflect the passage of the seasons but rather the speed of automobiles and airplanes. Caught in a metallic frenzy, the industrialized man is under constant and intense pressure. Interior tranquillity and meditation are forbidden to him. If this man is a musician, he will think like Stockhausen or Boulez; it is natural for him to seek new means of sonorous expression through electronics in order to represent a cultural condition humanity has never before experienced. Good-by clarinet, good-by violin; sing of roses and grassy trails. Our life is a dance in the cement streets, the smell of gasoline, and masses of people. We need other sounds to clothe our dreams.
>
> . . . Let us therefore be sympathetic to the work of Stockhausen, Boulez, and Nono, and to that of Pierre Schaeffer and Pierre Henry. But let us avoid the common mistake of thinking that theirs is the only path possible. There are still and there will always be people who have nothing to do with city life and who are not subjects of the industrial empire. We can even say that the great majority of men are not touched by the painful tensions

of our machine age. Their daily reality is still composed of blossoming apple trees and nocturnal calm. And they too have the right to express themselves, and their music has nothing in common with the works that tell of our new anxiety. Their calm is a blessing, as we know from Boris Blacher's lovely *Zweites Konzert für Klavier und Orchester,* op. 42, Werner Egk's *Sonata for Orchestra,* and the delightful a cappella composition, *Mörike Chorliederbuch,* op. 19, by Hugo Distler, dead before his time. They deserve our gratitude for their fresh spontaneity and their purity of soul.[3]

Spontaneity, purity of soul, and an earnest desire to preach God's Word through his music — these were indeed attributes of Hugo Distler. What lovelier tribute than the alto solo from a cantata text composed in honor of the 25th anniversary of the founding of the Lübeck *Sing- und Spielkreis* (June 1953), written by the Lübeck author Paul Brockhaus?

Your hour struck and you were driven forth
From your solitary world of creation into the vast life beyond;
The thorn of disquiet in your side,
You became for yourself, as life had become for you — never
    enough.

The bliss and necessity of creating
Were, to your salvation and destruction, bound deep within you.
We, however, think of the fleeting hours
When the flames of your soul glowed for us.

It glowed brilliantly for the joy of the world;
Now that you have entered eternal silence,
As we loved you, you remain our own:
An incandescent heart, which, in giving,
Expended itself.[4]

NOTES TO CHAPTER 4

1. Jan Bender, *Now Let All Loudly Sing Praise to God* (Concordia 97-6376, 1962).
2. Conversation with Siegfried Reda, Summer Academy for Organists, Haarlem, Holland, July 1964.
3. Paul Collaer, *A History of Modern Music,* translated by Sally Abeles (New York, 1961), pp. 398–400.
4. From *Festkantate* by Paul Brockhaus, IV. "Hugo Distler," text booklet presented to the author by KMD Bruno Grusnick, Lübeck, August 25, 1962. Translated, 1963, by Thomas Caldwell.

PHOTO ALBUM

The Church of St. Jakobi, Lübeck, from the southeast

The "Small" organ of St. Jakobi

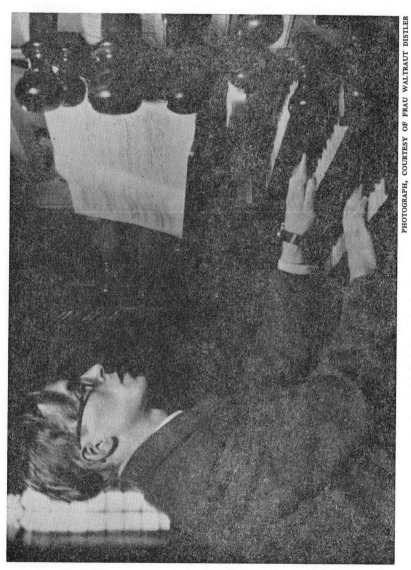

Distler at the rear gallery organ, St. Jakobi

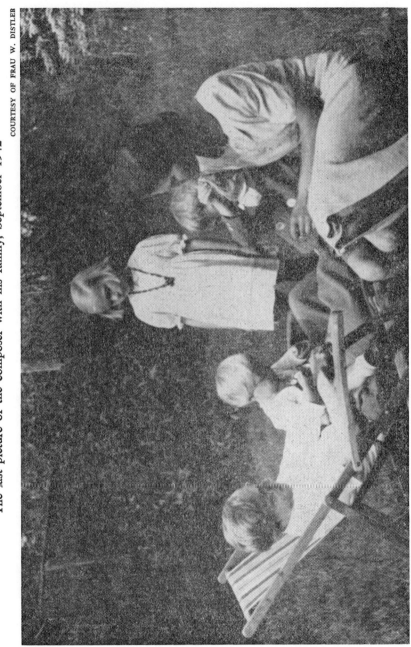

The last picture of the composer with his family, September 1942

The last photograph of the composer
September 1942, Strausberg bei Berlin

PROGRAMS OF THE VESPER SERVICES AT THE ST. JAKOBIKIRCHE LÜBECK, GERMANY, 1931—1937

Unless otherwise indicated, the choir at each program was the Lübeck *Sing- und Spielkreis*, conducted by Bruno Grusnick. Hugo Distler was the organist. Varying terminology may be noticed in these programs, as, for example, the use of both *Liturgie* and *Pastor* to denote the liturgical portions of the service; the original usage has been maintained throughout.

Vesper 1 [Feb. 15, 1931]

Orgel	Präludium und Fuge, e-moll	Buxtehude
Liturgie	Schriftverlesung und Lutherwort	
Gemeinde	Choral: "Erhalt uns, Herr, bei deinem Wort"	
	Vers "In dieser schwer'n, betrübten Zeit"	
Chor	Kyrie, *Missa Brevis*	Buxtehude
Orgel	Zwei Choralphantasien über "Erhalt uns, Herr"	Buxtehude
Chor	3-st. Kanon, "Herr, so du hilfst"	Caldara
Liturgie	Vaterunser und Friedensgruss	
Chor	Abendchoral (4-st.)	Vulpius
	"Hinunter ist der Sonnenschein"	
Gemeinde	Choral: "Erhalt uns, Herr"	
	Vers "Dein Wort ist unsers Herzens Trutz"	
Orgel	Präludium und Fuge, F-dur	Buxtehude

Vesper 2 [March 15, 1931]

Vokal- und Instrumentalsätze von Johann Sebastian Bach

Orgel	Fantasie, c-moll (5-st.)
Liturgie	Schriftverlesung und Lutherwort
Orgel	Choralvorspiel, "Vater unser im Himmelreich"
Gemeinde	Choral: "Vater unser"
Chor	Vers 2, "Gedenk an deins Sohns bittern Tod"
Gemeinde	Vers 3, "Ach, Herr, vergib"
Orgel	Sonate, e-moll
Chor	Aus der *h-moll Messe*, "Agnus Dei" mit Solo Violine und Orgel-continuo
Violine	Triosonate, d-moll (Adagio, Allegro, Largo, Vivace)

Orgel	Choral: "Herzlich tut mich verlangen"	
Gemeinde	Choral: "Ich danke dir von Herzen"	
Chor	Vers 2, "Wenn ich einmal soll scheiden"	
Gemeinde	Vers 3, "Erscheine mir zum Schilde"	
Liturgie	Vaterunser und Friedensgruss	
Orgel	Canzona, d-moll	

Mitwirkende: Gertrud Gädeke, Leopold Thieme, Violine

Vesper 3 [April 12, 1931]

Orgel	Präambulum in F	J. Praetorius
Liturgie	Schriftverlesung und Lutherwort	
Orgel	Choralvorspiel, "Christ lag in Todesban- den"	Scheidt
Gemeinde	Choral: "Christ lag"	
Chor	"Christ lag in Todesbanden"	Hassler
Gemeinde	Choral, Vers 3	
Orgel	Fantasia (*Tabulatura Nova*, II)	Scheidt
Duett	"Wo willst du hin, weil's Abend ist"	P. Krieger
Orgel	Choralvorspiel, "Christ lag"	Scheidt
Gemeinde	Vers "Es war ein wunderlicher Krieg"	
Chor	Vers "So feiern wir das hohe Fest"	
Gemeinde	Vers "Wir essen und leben wohl"	
Liturgie	Vaterunser und Friedensgruss	
Orgel	Toccata in C	Pachelbel

Mitwirkende: Cäcilie von der Hude, Sopran; Lotte Hansen, Alt

Vesper 4 [May 10, 1931]

Der Liturgische Chor der Landeskirche, Dr. Fritz Jung, Dir.

Orgel	Choralvorspiel, "Herr Christ, der einig Gotts Sohn"	Bach
Gemeinde	Choral: "Herr Christ"	
Chor	Vers 2	
Gemeinde	Vers 3	
Liturgie	Schriftverlesung und Väterwort	
Orgel	Präludium, Largo [sic] und Fuge	Bach
Chor	"Cantate Domino canticum novum"	Schütz
Orgel	Choralvorspiel, "Erschienen ist der herrlich Tag"	Bach
Gemeinde	Choral, "Erschienen ist"	
Chor	Vers 2	
Gemeinde	Vers 3	
Liturgie	Vaterunser und Friedensgruss	
Orgel	Pastorale in vier Sätzen, F-dur	Bach

Vesper 5 [June 7, 1931]

Vierhundertjahrfeier der Einführung der Reformation in Lübeck

Orgel	Drei Orgelpunkttoccaten	Pachelbel
Pastor	Schriftverlesung und Väterwort	
Orgel	Choralvorspiel, "Ein feste Burg"	Hanff
Chor	Choral, "Ein feste Burg"	K. Othmayr
Gemeinde	Choral, Vers 3	

166

Pastor	Lesung des 46. Psalms	
Orgel	Choralvorspiel, "Ein feste Burg"	Walther
Chor	Choral	Hassler
Gemeinde	Vers "Das Wort sie sollen lassen"	
Chor	Motette, "Ein feste Burg"	Hassler
Pastor	Vaterunser und Friedensgruss	
Orgel	Präludium und Fuge, e-moll	Bruhns

Vesper 6 [Oct. 4, 1931]

(Anlässlich nordisch-deutsche Orgelwoche, Lübeck)

Orgel	Lydische Toccata	E. Barthe
Pastor	Eingangswort und Lesung	
Orgel	"Aus tiefer Not" (Organistenamt)	Günther Ramin
Chor	Choral, "Aus tiefer Not"	Kurt Thomas
Gemeinde	Choral	
Chor	Eine deutsche Choralmesse, op. 3 Teil I (durch Lobgesang)	Distler
Orgel	Choralvorspiel (Antiphonie), "Wir glauben all"	Distler
Gemeinde	Choral, "Wir glauben all"	
Chor	Choralmesse, Teil II	
Orgel	Choralvorspiel, "Nun danket alle Gott" (Organistenamt)	Karl Hasse
Chor	Choral, "Nun danket"	Distler
Gemeinde	Choral, "Nun danket"	
Pastor	Vaterunser und Friedensgruss	
Orgel	Toccata	Walter Kraft

Vesper 7 [Nov. 1, 1931]

Orgel	Hymnus "O Lux beata trinitas"	M. Praetorius
Liturgie	Eingangswort und Lesung	
Orgel	Variationen über den Lutherchoral "Vater unser im Himmelreich"	Scheidt
Gemeinde	Choral, Vers 1	
Orgel	Choral, Vers 2 (c. f. im Tenor)	
Chor	Choral, Vers "Geheiligt werd der Name"	J. Weinmann
Orgel	Choral, Vers 3 (c. f. im Sopran)	
Gemeinde	Choral, Vers "Es komm dein Reich"	
Orgel	Choral, Vers 4 (Bicinium)	
Chor	Choral, Vers "Dein Will gescheh"	K. Othmayr
Orgel	Choral, Vers 5 (c. f. im Tenor)	
Chor	Choral, "Gib uns heut unser täglich Brot"	A. von Bruck
Orgel	Choral, Vers 6 (c. f. im Bass)	
Gemeinde	Choral, "All unsere Schuld"	
Orgel	Choral, Vers 7 (c. f. im Bass)	
Chor	"Führ uns, Herr, in Versuchung nicht"	J. de Vento
Orgel	Choral, Vers 8 (c. f. im Bass, koloriert)	
Chor	"Vom allem Übel uns erlös"	Hassler
Gemeinde	Choral, Vers "Amen"	
Liturgie	Vaterunser und Friedensgruss	
Orgel	Präludium und Fuge, E-dur	Lübeck

Vesper 8 [Nov. 29, 1931]

Orgel	Pastorale, F-dur	Bach
Liturgie	Lesungen: Heb. 10:35-37, 39; Offb. 3:20	
	Aus dem *Cherubinischen Wandersmann:*	
	IV/17, I/61, III/187, II/103,	
	IV/219, V/66	
Gemeinde	Choral, "Nun komm, der Heiden Heiland"	
Chor und		
Instrumente	*Kleine Adventsmusik, op. 4*	Distler
Gemeinde	Choral, Vers "Lob sei Gott"	
Pastor	Vaterunser und Friedensgruss	
Orgel	Präludium und Fuge, Es-dur	Bach

Mitwirkende: Konzertmeister K. Kundrat, Violine; Fr. König, Oboe; K. Luftmann, Flöte; H. Distler an der Orgel und am Cembalo

Vesper 9 [Dec. 27, 1931]

Werke von Dietrich Buxtehude

Orgel	"Lobt Gott, ihr Christen, allzugleich"
Gemeinde	Choral, "Lobt Gott"
Liturgie	Eingangswort und Lesung
Orgel	Fantasie in 2 Versen über "Wie schön leuchtet"
Kantate	"Lobet Christen, euren Heiland"
Liturgie	Bibelwort
Kantate	"Singet dem Herrn ein neues Lied"
Liturgie	Bibelwort
Chor	Das Magnificat für 5-st. Chor. Streicher und Generalbass
Liturgie	Vaterunser und Friedensgruss
Orgel	Präludium und Fuge, a-moll

Mitwirkende: Cäcilie von der Hude, Sopran; Konzertmeister K. Denker, Violine; Ein Streicherchor

Vesper 10 [Jan. 24, 1932]

Orgel	"Mein junges Leben hat ein End"	Sweelinck
Liturgie	Eingangswort und Lesung	
Gemeinde	Choral, "Nun sich der Tag geendet"	
	Weise: "Nun ruhen alle Wälder"	
Kinderchor	Dreistimmige Lieder	K. Othmayr
	"Ach Gott, vom Himmel sieh darein"	
	"Wär' Gott nicht bei uns diese Zeit"	
	"Herr Christ, der einig Gotts Sohn"	
Orgel	Choralpartita in 12 Versen	Scheidt
	"Warum betrübst du dich, mein Herz?"	
Kinderchor	Dreistimmige Lieder	Distler
	"Nun bitten wir den Heiligen Geist"	
	"In Gottes Namen fahren wir"	
	"Vater unser im Himmelreich"	
Gemeinde	Choral, Vers "Dass du mich stets umgibest"	
Liturgie	Vaterunser und Friedensgruss	
Orgel	Credo in unum Deum	Scheidt

Mitwirkende: Der Kinderchor von St. Jakobi unter Leitung von Hugo Distler

Vesper 11 [Feb. 21, 1932]

Orgel	Partita, "Sei gegrüsset, Jesu gütig"	Bach
Chor	Kyrie, "Deutsche Messe"	Schütz
Liturgie	Lesung	
Orgel	"Herzlich tut mich verlangen"	Bach
Gemeinde	Choralvers	
Chor	Choralvers	
Gemeinde	Choralvers	
Chor	6-st. Motette, "Selig sind die Toten"	Schütz
Orgel	Fantasie und Fuge, g-moll	Bach
Liturgie	Vaterunser und Friedensgruss	
Chor	Amen	

Vesper 12 [March 25, 1932]

Orgel	"Kyrie, Gott Vater in Ewigkeit,"	Bach
	Klavierübung, III	
Liturgie	Lesungen	
Orgel	Choralvorspiel, "Herzlich tut"	Buxtehude
Gemeinde	Choral, "O Haupt voll Blut und Wunden"	
Orgel	"Christe, aller Welt Trost"	Bach
Chor	Matthäus-Passion	Schütz
Liturgie	Vaterunser und Friedensgruss	
Orgel	"Kyrie, Gott, Heiliger Geist"	Bach

Vesper 13 [April 24, 1932]

Orgel	"Allein Gott in der Höh' sei Ehr' "	Bach
Chor	"Allein Gott"	Schröter
Liturgie	Lesung	
Orgel	Choralvorspiel, "Allein Gott"	Bach
Gemeinde	Choral, 2 Verse	
Chor	Cantate Domino	Buxtehude
Orgel	Präludium, Largo und Fuge, C-dur	Bach
Liturgie	Vaterunser und Friedensgruss	
Chor	Amen	Schütz

Vesper 14 [May 29, 1932]

Orgel	Toccata und Fuge, d-moll	Bach
Chor	"Bringt Ehr und Preis dem Herrn"	Schütz
Liturgie	Eingangsspruch	
Orgel	"Nun bitten wir den Heiligen Geist"	Buxtehude
Chor	"Nun bitten wir"	Distler
Gemeinde	Choral, Vers 3	
Liturgie	Lesung	
Orgel	"Nun bitten wir"	Buxtehude
Chor	Choral, Vers "Du süsse Lieb"	Distler
Gemeinde	Choral, Vers "Du höchster Tröster"	
Chor	Aus der *Geistlichen Chormusik,* 1648	Schütz
	"Die Himmel erzählen die Ehre Gottes"	
Orgel	"Herr Christ, der einig Gotts Sohn"	Bach
Gemeinde	Choral, Vers "Du Schöpfer aller Dinge"	
Liturgie	Vaterunser und Friedensgruss	
Orgel	Präludium, Fuge und Chaconne, C-dur	Buxtehude

Vesper 15 [Nov. 6, 1932]

Chorwerke von Heinrich Schütz (1585, gestorben 6. November, 1672)
und *Orgelwerke von Johann Pachelbel* (1653—1706)

Orgel	Präludium, Fuge und Chaconne, d-moll
Pastor	Eingangswort
Gemeinde	Choral, "Der Tag hat sich geneiget"
	Weise: Schütz
Chor	Choral, Vers "Nichts ist auf dieser Erden"
Gemeinde	Choral, Vers "Ich bitt, dass du mir gnädig"
Solo	Aus den *kleinen geistlichen Konzerten*
	"Ich liege und schlafe und erwache"
Chor	Kyrie, *Deutsche Messe*
Solo	"Ich will den Herren loben allezeit"
Pastor	Lesung
Solo	"Bringt her dem Herrn"
Chor	"Die Himmel erzählen" (6-st.)
Gemeinde	Choral, "Ich weiss, woran ich glaube"
	Weise: Schütz
Chor	Choral, Vers 2
Gemeinde	Choral, Vers 3
Pastor	Vaterunser und Friedensgruss
Chor	Amen (Satz: Schütz)
Orgel	Drei Orgelpunkttoccaten

Mitwirkender: Hans Meyer, Berlin, Gesang

Vesper 16 [Nov. 27, 1932]

Die Kantorei an St. Jakobi, Gemischter Chor und Kinderchor unter Leitung
von Hugo Distler; an der historischen Orgel: Käte Derlien und Hugo Distler.

Orgel	Pastorale, F-dur	Bach
Pastor und		
Chor	Magnificat	
Orgel	Orgelchoral, "Nun komm, der Heiden	
	Heiland"	Scheidt
Chor	Choral, Vers 1 (4-st.)	Resinarius
Gemeinde	Choral, Vers 2	
Pastor	Lesung: Lucas 1:26-32a; 36a; 37-38	
Orgel	Orgelchoral, "Nun komm"	Buxtehude
Chor	Choral, Vers 3 (2-st.)	Othmayer
Pastor	Lesung: Lucas 1:39-40; 41b-43; 45	
Orgel	Orgelchoral, "Nun komm"	Pachelbel
Chor	Choral, Vers 4 (4-st.)	Osiander
Gemeinde	Choral, Vers 5	
Pastor	Lesung: Lucas 1:46-50	
Orgel	Orgelchoral, "Nun komm"	A. Kniller
Chor	Choral, Vers 6 (3-st.)	M. Praetorius
Pastor	Lesung: Johannes 1:14-16	
Orgel	Orgelchoral, "Nun komm"	Zachow
Chor	Choral, Vers 7 (4-st.)	Hassler
Gemeinde	Choral, Vers 8	
Chor	Aus der *Geistlichen Chormusik*	
	"Es ist erschienen die heilsame Gnade"	Schütz
Pastor	Vaterunser und Friedensgruss	
Orgel	Choralfantasie, "Nun komm"	Bach

170

Vesper 17 [Dec. 26, 1932]

Orgel	Präludium, Largo und Fuge, C-dur	Bach
Chor	"Nun freut euch"	Bened. Ducis
Pastor	Eingangswort und Lesung	
Orgel	Vorspiel, "In dulci jubilo"	Walther
Chor	In dulci jubilo (2-, 3-st.)	Praetorius
Gemeinde	Choral, Vers 3	
Chor	Choral (4-st.)	Praetorius
Gemeinde	Choral, Vers 5	
Chor	"Hört zu und seid getrost"	Schröter
	"Geboren ist uns Immanuel"	Praetorius
Orgel	Vorspiel, "Lobt Gott, ihr Christen"	Buxtehude
Gemeinde	Choral	
Chor	Choral (4-st.)	Schröter
Gemeinde	Choral, Vers 3	
Orgel	Partita, "Nun komm, der Heiden Heiland"	Distler
Pastor	Vaterunser und Segen	
Chor	Amen	
Gemeinde	Choral, "Lobt Gott, ihr Christen"	
	Vers "Heut' schleusst er wieder auf die Tür"	

Unter dem Nachspiel der Orgel verlässt die Gemeinde die Kirche. Kirche geheizt.

Vesper 18 [Feb. 26, 1933]

Kirchenmusik der Gegenwart

Sing- und Spielkreis unter Leitung von Bruno Grusnick; Der Kinderchor von St. Jakobi unter Leitung von Hugo Distler; Paul Uthgennant und Karl Hessen, Oboen

Orgel	Toccata über ABA	Walter Kraft
Chor	Kyrie für 3 gleiche Stimmen	Carriere
Liturgie	Eingangswort	
Orgel	Vorspiel	
Gemeinde	Choral, "Was mein Gott will, gescheh allzeit"	
Kinder	Motetten	Distler
	"Wo Gott zum Haus nicht gibt sein Gunst"	
	"Ein neu Gebot gebe ich euch"	
Liturgie	Lesung	
Chor	"Herr, wie du willst, so schick's mit mir"	Kurt Thomas
Liturgie	Lesung	
Chor	Kleine geistliche Abendmusik für 3-st. gemischten Chor, 2 Oboen und Cembalo	Distler
Orgel	Vorspiel	
Gemeinde	Choral, "Drum will ich gern von dieser Welt"	
Liturgie	Vaterunser und Friedensgruss	
Orgel	Ricercar in 3 Sätzen	Walter Kraft

Vesper 19 [March 12, 1933]

Orgel	Chaconne, e-moll	Buxtehude
Chor	Aus den *Musikalischen Exequien*	Schütz

	"Nacket bin ich vom Mutterleibe kommen"	
	"... Christus ist mein Leben"	
	"... Leben wir, so leben wir dem Herrn"	
Liturgie	Eingangswort	
Gemeinde	Choral, "Die Herrlichkeit der Erden"	
Liturgie	Lesung (Luther)	
Orgel	"Mein junges Leben hat ein End"	Sweelinck
Liturgie	Lesung (aus den Briefen gefallener Studenten)	
Chor	"Selig sind die Toten"	Schütz
Gemeinde	Choral, "Wenn mein Stündlein vorhanden ist"	
Chor	Choral, Vers 2	
Gemeinde	Choral, Vers 3	
Chor	"So fahr ich hin zu Jesu Christ"	Schütz
Liturgie	Vaterunser und Friedensgruss	
Orgel	Präludium und Fuge, g-moll	Buxtehude

Vesper 20 [April 14, 1933]

Orgel	Toccata, c-moll	Pachelbel
Liturgie	Eingangswort und Lesung	
Orgel	"Herzlich tut mich verlangen"	Bach
Gemeinde	Choral, "O Haupt voll Blut und Wunden"	
Chor	Matthäus-Passion	Schütz
Orgel	"Herzlich tut"	Walther
Gemeinde	Choral, Vers "Wenn ich einmal soll scheiden"	
Pastor	Vaterunser und Friedensgruss	
Gemeinde	Choral, Vers "Erscheine mir zum Schilde"	

Vesper 21 [May 21, 1933]

Orgel	Ricercare, c-moll	Pachelbel
Liturgie	Eingangswort und Lesung	
Gemeinde	Choral, "Lob Gott getrost mit Singen"	
Liturgie	Lesung	
Orgel	Fuge, C-dur	Pachelbel
Chor	Cantate Domino	Buxtehude
Orgel	Toccata, C-dur	Pachelbel
Chor	"Herr Gott, dich loben wir"	Distler
Gemeinde	Choral, "Gott sollen wir billig loben"	
Liturgie	Vaterunser und Friedensgruss	
Orgel	Canzona, d-moll	Bach

Vesper 22 [Nov. 5, 1933]

Alle Chöre und Chorbearbeitungen stammen von Hugo Distler

Lübecker Sing- und Spielkreis, Die St. Jakobi Kantorei

Orgel	Präludium, Es-dur	Bach
Gemeinde	Choral, "Lobe den Herren"	
Chor	Kleine Choralmotette, "Lobe den Herren"	
Gemeinde	Choral, Vers 3	
Chor	Antiphon, "Gott ist unsre Zuversicht"	

172

Pastor	Psalmodie, "Ist Gott für mich"	
Chor	Antiphon	
Pastor	Lesung	
Gemeinde	Choral, "Wach auf, du deutsches Land"	
Chor	Choral, Vers 2	
Gemeinde	Choral, Vers 3	
Pastor	Lesung	
Chor	Antiphon, "Gott sei Lob und Ehre"	
Pastor	Psalmodie, "Meine Seele erhebt Gott" (Magnificat)	
Chor	Antiphon	
Pastor	Vaterunser und Friedensgruss	
Orgel	Tripelfuge, Es-dur	Bach

Vesper 23 [Dec. 26, 1933]

Orgel	Vorspiel, "Lobt Gott, ihr Christen, allzugleich"	Buxtehude
Gemeinde	Choral, "Lobt Gott, ihr Christen"	
Pastor	Eingangswort	
Orgel	Präludium und Fuge, G-dur	Bach
Chor	Die Weihnachtsgeschichte, op. 10	Distler
Pastor	Vaterunser und Friedensgruss	
Orgel	Toccata, C-dur	Pachelbel

Vesper 24 [Feb. 25, 1934]

Orgel	"Wenn mein Stündlein vorhanden ist"	Pachelbel
Pastor	Eingangswort und Lesung	
Gemeinde	Choral, "Wenn mein Stündlein"	
Chor	Deutsche Sprüche von Leben und Tod	Lechner
Orgel	"Mein junges Leben hat ein End"	Sweelinck
Chor	Aus der *Geistlichen Chormusik*, 1648 "Selig sind die Toten"	Schütz
Gemeinde	Choral, Verse 3 und 4	
Pastor	Vaterunser und Friedensgruss	
Orgel	Präludium und Fuge, E-dur	Lübeck

Vesper 25 [March 30, 1934]

Orgel	"Herzlich tut mich verlangen"	Bach
Gemeinde	Choral, "O Haupt voll Blut und Wunden"	
Pastor	Eingangswort und Lesung	
Gemeinde	Choral, Vers "Ich will hier bei dir stehen"	
Chor	Matthäus-Passion	Schütz
Gemeinde	Choral, Verse 3 und 4	
Pastor	Vaterunser und Friedensgruss	
Orgel	Fantasia, g-moll	Pachelbel

Vesper 26 [April 29, 1934]

Orgel	Präludium und Fuge, D-dur	Buxtehude
Pastor	Eingangswort	
Gemeinde	Choral, "Lobt Gott in allen Landen" Weise: "Lobt Gott getrost mit Singen"	
Chor	"Lobe den Herren," kleine Motette	Distler
Pastor	Lesung	

173

Gemeinde	Choral, "Lobt Gott getrost mit Singen"	
Chor	"Singet dem Herrn ein neues Lied"	Distler
Gemeinde	Choral, "Gott solln wir billig Loben"	
Pastor und		
Gemeinde	Te Deum (im Wechselgesang)	
Pastor	Vaterunser und Friedensgruss	
Orgel	Präludium und Fuge, C-dur	Bach

Vesper 27 [June 3, 1934]

Orgel	Toccata und Fuge	Pachelbel
Pastor	Eingangswort und Lesung	
Gemeinde	Choral, "Herr Christ, der einig Gotts Sohn"	
Chor	Aus der *Geistlichen Chormusik,* 1648 "Ich bin ein rechter Weinstock"	Schütz
Gemeinde	Choral, "Lass uns in deiner Liebe"	
Chor	Aus den *Psalmen für Doppelchor* "Singet dem Herrn ein neues Lied"	Schütz
Gemeinde	Choral, Vers "Du Schöpfer aller Dinge"	
Pastor	Vaterunser und Friedensgruss	
Orgel	Toccata, F-dur	Bach

Vesper 28 [Jan. 6, 1935]

(no program preserved)

Distler's *Weihnachtsgeschichte,* opus 10

Vesper 29 [April 19, 1935]

(no program preserved)

The *Matthäus-Passion* by Heinrich Schütz

Vesper 30 [Nov. 24, 1935]

Geistliche Abendmusik mit Werken von Hugo Distler

Orgel	Ricercare in d-moll
Chor	*Kurze Messe:* Kyrie und Gloria
Liturgie	Eingangsspruch und erste Lesung
Chor	"Ich wollt, dass ich daheime wär"
Orgel	Choralvorspiel, "Ach wie flüchtig, ach wie nichtig"
Gemeinde	Choral, "Ach wie flüchtig"
Chor	Aus der *Geistlichen Chormusik,* op. 12 "Totentanz" Motette
Liturgie	Zweite Lesung
Chor	Aus der *Geistlichen Chormusik* Motette "Wachet auf"
Gemeinde	Choral, "Wachet auf"
Liturgie	Dritte Lesung, Vaterunser, Segen
Orgel	Partita über "Wachet auf"

Vesper 31 [Dec. 26, 1935]

Orgel	Choralfantasie "Nun freut euch"	Buxtehude
Pastor	Eingangswort	

Gemeinde	Choral, "Nun freut euch"	
Pastor	Lesung	
Chor	Die Weihnachtsgeschichte, op. 10	Distler
Pastor	Schlusswort, Vaterunser und Friedensgruss	
Chor	Amen	
Gemeinde	Choral, "Lobt Gott, ihr Christen, allzu-gleich"	
Chor	Choral, Vers 5	
Gemeinde	Choral, Wiederholung, Vers 5	

Vesper 32 [Jan. 19, 1936]

An der Orgel: Professor Fritz Heitmann (Berlin)

Orgel	Präludium, e-moll	Bruhns
Pastor	Eingangswort und Lesung	
Chor	"Ich will sehr hoch erheben dich"	Schütz
Orgel	Choralvorspiel, "Nun lasst uns Gott, dem Herren"	Lübeck
Gemeinde	Choral, "Nun lasst uns Gott"	
Orgel	"Wie schön leuchtet der Morgenstern"	Buxtehude
Chor	"Das ist je gewisslich wahr"	Schütz
Orgel	Präludium und Fuge, D-dur	Buxtehude
Pastor	Lesung	
Orgel	Vorspiel, "Nun lasst uns Gott"	Lübeck
Gemeinde	Choralvers	
Pastor	Vaterunser und Friedensgruss	
Orgel	Fantasie und Fuge, g-moll	Bach

Vesper 33 [Feb. 16, 1936]

Chor der Hamburger Volksmusikschule, unter Leitung von Walter Kraft. An der kleinen Orgel, Hugo Distler

Orgel	"Wie schön leuchtet der Morgenstern"	Distler
Gemeinde	Choral, "Wie schön leuchtet"	
Chor	3-st. Chorsatz aus *Spandauer Chorbuch* "O Jesu, süsses Licht"	Pepping
Pastor	Eingangswort	
Orgel	Choralpartita, "Wie schön leuchtet"	Pepping
Gemeinde	Choral, Verse 2 und 3	
Chor	7-st. Motette über einen *c. f.* aus dem *Handbuch der deutschen ev. Kirchenmusik* "Hallelujah! Singt und seid froh"	Walter Kraft
Pastor	Lesung	
Chor	10-st. Chorsatz für 2 Chöre "Wie schön leuchtet"	Walter Kraft
Gemeinde	Choral	
Pastor	Vaterunser und Friedensgruss	
Orgel	Chaconne, g-moll	Distler

Vesper 34 [March 8, 1936]

An beiden Orgeln: Domkantor Hans Heintze (Dresden)

Gr. Orgel	Präludium und Fuge, a-moll	Bach
Pastor	Eingangswort und Lesung	

Gemeinde	Choral, "Wenn mein Stündlein vorhanden ist"	
Kl. Orgel	Partita, "Ach wie flüchtig"	Böhm
Chor	Deutsche Sprüche von Leben und Tod	Lechner
Kl. Orgel	Triosonate, e-moll	Bach
Pastor	Lesung	
Gemeinde	Choral, Verse 3 und 4	
Pastor	Vaterunser und Friedensgruss	
Kl. Orgel	Präludium und Fuge, G-dur	Bruhns

Vesper 35 [April 10, 1936]

Orgel	Fantasie, g-moll	Pachelbel
Pastor	Eingangswort und Lesung	
Orgel	"O Haupt voll Blut und Wunden"	Bach
Gemeinde	Choral, "O Haupt," 2 Verse	
Chor	Matthäus-Passion	Schütz
Gemeinde	Choral, Verse 3 und 4	
Pastor	Vaterunser und Friedensgruss	
Orgel	Fantasie, e-moll	Bach

Vesper 36 [Nov. 1, 1936]

Orgel	"Aus tiefer Not"	Bach
Pastor	Eingangswort	
Gemeinde	Choral, "Aus tiefer Not"	
Chor	Busspsalm, 6-st.	A. Gabrieli
	"Domine, ne in furore tuo arguas me"	
Pastor	Lesung	
Orgel	Toccata, Adagio und Fuge	Bach
Chor	Motette, "Herr, auf dich traue ich"	Schütz
Gemeinde	Choral, "Nun freut euch"	
Chor	Motette, "Das ist je gewisslich wahr"	Schütz
Gemeinde	Choral, "Nun freut euch"	
Pastor	Vaterunser und Segen	
Orgel	Präludium und Tripelfuge, Es-dur	Bach

Vesper 37 [Nov. 29, 1936]

Orgel	Tokkata (1936)	Jan Bender
Liturgie und Chor	Lobgesang Mariä (Magnificat)	
Chor	"Nun freut euch" (1935)	Distler
Orgel	Choralvorspiel, "Nun komm, der Heiden Heiland" (1931)	Distler
Gemeinde	Choral, "Nun komm"	
Orgel	Aus der Partita "Nun komm" (1933)	Distler
Chor	Kleine Adventsmusik, op. 4	Distler
Chor	Choral, "Nun freut euch"	
Liturgie	Vaterunser und Segen	
Chor	Amen (1933)	Distler
Orgel	Chaconne und Tokkata aus der Partita "Nun komm, der Heiden Heiland"	Distler

Vesper 38 [Dec. 27, 1936]

An der Orgel: Ika Bräck

Orgel	Präludium, G-dur	Bach
Pastor	Eingangswort und Lesung	
Gemeinde	Choral, "Gelobet seist du, Jesu Christ"	
Chor	Die Weihnachtsgeschichte, op. 10	Distler
Gemeinde	Choral, "So singen wir all Amen"	
Pastor	Vaterunser und Friedensgruss	
Chor	Tripel Amen	Distler
Orgel	Fuge, G-dur	Bach

THE PUBLISHED WORKS OF HUGO DISTLER

Op. 1	Konzertante Sonate für 2 Klaviere	Breitkopf
Op. 2	Choralmotette "Herzlich lieb hab' ich dich, o Herr"	Breitkopf
Op. 3	Eine deutsche Choralmesse	Breitkopf
Op. 4	Kleine Adventsmusik	Breitkopf
Op. 5	Der Jahrkreis	BA 676
Op. 6/I	Kleine geistliche Abendmusik: "Christ, der du bist der helle Tag"	BA 636
Op. 6/II	Drei kleine Choralmotetten	
	Lobe den Herren	BA 589
	Es ist das Heil uns kommen her	BA 586,87
	Komm, Heiliger Geist, Herre Gott	BA 588
Op. 7	Choralpassion	BA 633
Op. 8/I	Orgelpartita, "Nun komm, der Heiden Heiland"	BA 637
Op. 8/II	Orgelpartita, "Wachet auf, ruft uns die Stimme"	BA 883
Op. 8/III	Kleine Orgelchoral-Bearbeitungen	BA 1222
Op. 9/I	Das Lied von der Glocke	
Op. 9/II	An die Natur (Weltliche Kantate)	BA 683
Op. 10	Die Weihnachtsgeschichte	BA 690
Op. 11/I	Wo Gott zum Haus nit gibt sein Gunst	BA 750
Op. 11/II	Nun danket all und bringet Ehr	BA 758
Op. 12	Geistliche Chormusik	
	Singet dem Herrn ein neues Lied	BA 751
	Totentanz	BA 752
	Wach auf, du deutsches Reich	BA 753
	Singet frisch und wohlgemut	BA 754
	Ich wollt, dass ich daheime wär	BA 755
	Wachet auf, ruft uns die Stimme	BA 756
	In der Welt habt ihr Angst	BA 757
	Das ist je gewisslich wahr	BA 1801
	Fürwahr, er trug unsere Krankheit	BA 1802
Op. 13	Liturgische Sätze über altevangelische Kyrie- und Gloriaweisen	BA 884
Op. 14	Konzert für Cembalo und Streichorchester	BA 1000
Op. 15a	Sonate für zwei Geigen und Klavier	BA 1091
Op. 15b	Elf kleine Klavierstücke für die Jugend	BA 1803
Op. 16	Neues Chorliederbuch	
	1. Bauernlieder	BA 1056
	2. Minnelieder I	BA 1057
	3. Minnelieder II	BA 1058
	4. Kalendersprüche I	BA 1059

CONCORDIA EDITIONS OF MUSIC
BY HUGO DISTLER

A Little Advent Music
I Wish That I Were Going Home
We Now Implore God the Holy Ghost
        (Contained in *A Second Morning Star Choir Book*)
Lord, Keep Us Steadfast in Thy Word
        (Contained in *The Hymn of the Week* — SAB, Part V)
The Christmas Story
Dear Christians, One and All, Rejoice
Praise God the Lord, Ye Sons of Men
Praise to the Lord, the Almighty
        (in the collection *A First Motet Book*)
A Selection of 18 motets from "Der Jahrkreis"

BIBLIOGRAPHY

Bergman, G. "Het Orgeloeuvre van Hugo Distler," *Mens en Melodie,* XII (1957), 310—314.

Bieske, W. "Die Orgelwerke Hugo Distlers," *Musik und Kirche,* XXII (1952), 177—181.

Blankenburg, W. "Besprechung des Jahrkreises," *Zeitschrift für Hausmusik,* Neue Folge von Collegium Musicum, Heft 5/6, 1933.

————. "Die Gegenwartslage der evangelischen Kirchenmusik," *Musik und Kirche,* XVII (1947), 33—39.

————. "Neue Wege im Choralsatz," *Musik und Kirche,* VII (1935), 16—21.

————. "Neue Kultusmusik — zum Erscheinen der liturgischen Sätze von Hugo Distler über altevangelische Kyrie- und Gloriaweisen," *Musik und Kirche,* VIII (1936), 247—253.

Bornefeld, H. "Hugo Distler," *Musica,* I (1947), 142—147.

————. "Orgelbau und neue Orgelmusik," *Musik und Kirche,* XXII (1952), Beiheft.

————. "Schöpferischer Historismus," *Musica,* XII (1958), 319—322.

Borris, S. *Über Wesen und Werden der neuen modernen Musik.* Halle an der Saale, n. d.

Bosse, B. *Hugo Distlers Bedeutung für die moderne Chorerziehung.* Celle, 1949.

Brodde, O. "Junge Kirchenmusik: Hugo Distler," *Deutsches Pfarrerblatt,* No. 38 (Sept. 21, 1937).

————. "Hugo Distlers Choralpassion in Hamburg," *Musik und Kirche,* XX (1950), 106—107.

Buelow, P. "Hugo-Distler-Tage in Lübeck," *Zeitschrift für Musik,* CXIV (1935), 239—240.

Collaer, P. *A History of Modern Music.* Trans. Sally Abeles. Cleveland and New York, 1961.

Demuth, N. *Musical Trends in the Twentieth Century.* London, 1952.

Distler, H. *Die beiden Orgeln in St. Jakobi zu Lübeck nach dem Umbau 1935.* Lübeck, 1935.

————. *Funktionelle Harmonielehre.* Kassel, 1942.

————. "Gedanken zum Problem der Registrierung alter, spezial Bachscher Orgelmusik," *Musik und Kirche,* XX (1937), 101—106.

————. "J. S. Bachs Dorische Toccata und Fuge," *Musik und Kirche,* XII (1940), 49—57.

————. "Die Orgel unsrer Zeit (1933)," *Musica,* I (1947), 147—153.

————. "Über seine 'Spielmusik für Positiv,' " *Hausmusik,* XVI (1952), 159—161.

————. "Vom Geiste der neuen evangelischen Kirchenmusik," *Zeitschrift für Musik,* CII (1935), 1325—1329.

"Distler in Japan: Lied am Herde," *Musica,* X (1956), 535—536.

Drummond, A. *German Protestantism since Luther.* London, 1951.

Duncan-Jones, A. *The Struggle for Religious Freedom in Germany.* London, 1938.

Erpf, H. *Vom Wesen der neuen Musik.* Stuttgart, 1950.

Gehring, P. "Distler's Organ Works," *The American Organist,* XLVI (1963), No. 7, 14—18.

Goebels, F. ". . . den Alltag zu erhölen," *Hausmusik,* XXIII (1959), 37—41.

Grabner, H. "Erinnerungen an Hugo Distler," unpublished memoir, n. d.

Grusnick, B. "Hugo Distlers Choralpassion," *Musik und Kirche,* V (1933), 39—43.

————. "Hugo Distler und Hermann Grabner," *Musica,* XVIII (1964), 55—65.

————. "Hugo Distler und wir," *Hausmusik,* XVI (1952), 153—159.

————. "Hugo Distler zum Gedächtnis," *Lübeckische Blätter,* 1942, 18 and 1952, 162 f.

————. "Wie Hugo Distler Jakobiorganist in Lübeck wurde," *Musik und Kirche,* XXVIII (1958), 97—107.

Hamel, P. "Orgelweihe in St. Jakobi," *Deutsche Allgemeine Zeitung,* Nov. 1, 1935.

————. Über die Interpretation Bachscher Orgelwerke," *Musik und Kirche,* XII (1940), 71—72.

Heidbrink, E. *Die Choralpassion von Hugo Distler:* Ein zeitgenössisches Werk und seine geistigen Bezüge zu historischen Vorbildern. Unpublished dissertation presented to the Staatliche Prüfungskommission für das künstlerische Lehramt an höheren Schulen, Freiburg, Spring, 1958.

Hennings, J. "Lübeckisches Kammerorchester," *Lübeckische Blätter,* 74 (1932), 287.

Herman, S. *It's Your Souls We Want.* New York, 1943.

————. *The Rebirth of the German Church.* New York, 1946.

Herzfeld, F. *Musica nova: Die Tonwelt unseres Jahrhunderts.* Berlin, 1953.

Hoffmann, H. "Die Sprache als Grundlage des Chorsingens," *Musik und Kirche,* IX (1937), 196—212; 247—258.

————. *Vom Wesen der zeitgenössischen Kirchenmusik.* Kassel, 1949.

Kappner, G. "In Memoriam Hugo Distler," *Musik und Gottesdienst,* XII (1958), 78—85.

"Kasseler Musiktage, 1935," *Lied und Volk,* V, No. 8 (November 1935), 96.

Kempff, G. *Der Kirchengesang im Lutherischen Gottesdienst und seine Erneuerung.* 1937.

Kessler, F. *Neue Bestrebungen auf dem Gebiet des Orgelchorals* (J. N.

David, Hugo Distler, E. Pepping). Unpublished dissertation, University of Mainz (Germany), 1949.

Kienlin, E. "Erinnerungen an Hugo Distler," *Hausmusik,* XXII (1958), 41—43.

"Kirchenchorarbeit im Kriege," *Kirchenchordienst,* VII (1942), bound in *Musik und Kirche,* XIII (1941).

Klein, K. "In Memoriam Hugo Distler," *Musica,* VI (1952), 451—454.

Klotz, H. "Die zweite Freiburger Orgeltagung 1938," *Musik und Kirche,* X (1938), 137 ff.

Klump, G. "A Brief Analysis of the Partita *Wachet auf, ruft uns die Stimme* by Hugo Distler," program notes for Eastman School of Music Lecture Recital, August 4, 1961.

Kolodin, I. "The New German Music," *Saturday Review,* Feb. 23, 1957, pp. 43 ff.

Kühl, A. W. "Vesper in St. Jakobi," *Lübeckische Blätter,* 73 (1931), 86.

Kwasnik, W. "The Organ Movement Is Already Declining," *The American Organist* (March 1962), 17.

Lange, M. "Hugo Distler in Memoriam," *Musica,* VI (1952), 478—479.

Laux, K. "Hugo Distler," *Musik und Musiker der Gegenwart,* I (1949).

Lehmann-Haupt, H. *Art Under a Dictatorship.* New York, 1954.

Leiper, H. *The Church-State Struggle in Germany* (a personal view based on two months' intimate contact with the situation in Europe during August and September 1934). New York, 1934.

Maack, R. "Orgeltage in Lübeck," *Musik und Kirche,* IV (1932), 246.

Machlis, J. *Introduction to Contemporary Music.* New York, 1961.

Mahrenholz, C. "Fünfzehn Jahre Orgelbewegung," *Musik und Kirche,* X (1938), 8—28.

Mersmann, H. *Die moderne Musik seit der Romantik.* Buecken, 1928.

Moser, H. *Die evangelische Kirchenmusik in Deutschland.* Berlin, 1953—54.

———. *Musik in Zeit und Raum.* Berlin, 1960.

Mudde, W. "De Componist Hugo Distler," *Mens en Melodie* (1950), 254—257.

———. "Hugo Distler-Gedanken in Mühlheim," *Musik und Kirche,* XXIII (1953), 164—165.

Mueller, K. "Die Neuordnung des Gottesdienstes in Theologie und Kirche," *Theologie und Liturgie,* 1952, pp. 197 ff.

Neumann, R. *The Pictorial History of the Third Reich.* New York, 1952.

Niebergall, A. *Evangelischer Gottesdienst heute.* Kassel, 1953.

Nievergelt, E. "Zeitgenössische evangelische Kirchenmusik," *Musik und Gottesdienst,* VI (1952), 161—169.

Osthoff, H. *Das deutsche Chorlied vom 16. Jahrhundert bis zur Gegenwart.* Köln, 1955.

Palmer, L. "Hugo Distler Twenty Years Later," *The Diapason* (November 1962), p. 8.

Peinen, B. von. "Kirchenmusik im Dritten Reich," *Musik und Kirche,* V (1953), 174—189.

Pfister, A. "Der Choral in der zeitgenössischen Orgelmusik," *Musik und Gottesdienst*, VI (1952), 76—80.

Power, M. *Religion in the Reich.* London, 1939.

Ramin, C. *Günther Ramin, ein Lebensbericht.* Freiburg i. Br., 1958.

Ramin, G. *Gedanken zur Klärung des Orgelproblems.* Kassel, 1929.

————. "Stil und Manier (Betrachtungen zur Wiedergabe der Orgelmusik verschiedener Zeiten)," *Musik und Kirche,* IX (1937), 212 to 216.

Rauchhaupt, U. von. *Die vokale Kirchenmusik Hugo Distlers.* (Die liturgische Praxis an St. Jakobi in Lübeck von 1930 bis 1937 und Distlers Kompositionsstil in ihrem wechselseitigen Verhältnis, dargestellt an ausgewählten Beispielen). Gütersloh, 1963.

Rutz, H. "In Memoriam Hugo Distler," *Musica,* X (1956), 101 f.

Schlink, E. *Zum theologischen Problem der Musik.* Tübingen, 1947.

Schmitt, U. *Hugo Distler und die frühe evangelische Kirchenmusik.* Unpublished dissertation, Heidelberg University (Germany), 1955.

Schmolzi, H. "Die Wort-Ton-Verhältnisse in Distlers Choralpassion," *Musica,* VII (1953), 556—561.

Schweinsberg, K. "Hugo Distler zum Gedächtnis," *Musik und Kirche,* XVI (1943), 28—34.

————. "Hugo Distlers 'Kalendersprüche,' op. 16," *Hausmusik,* VII (1938), 107—111.

Shirer, W. *The Rise and Fall of the Third Reich.* New York, 1960. Paperback, New York, 1962.

Sitwell, E. *Collected Poems of Edith Sitwell.* New York, 1954.

Sitwell, O. *Those Were the Days: Panorama with Figures.* London, 1938.

Slonimsky, N. *Music Since 1900.* 3d ed., New York, 1949.

Smets, P. *Die historischen Orgelwerke der Stadt Lübeck.* Mainz, 1945.

Söhngen, O. "Die Erneuerung der Kirchenmusik in Deutschland," *Musik und Gottesdienst,* III (1949), 1—8.

————. *Kämpfende Kirchenmusik: Die Bewährungsprobe der evangelischen Kirchenmusik im Dritten Reich.* Kassel, 1954.

————. "Kirche und zeitgenössische Kirchenmusik," *Musik und Kirche,* IV (1932), 193—222.

————. "Kirchenmusik im Dritten Reich," *Die Kirche* (1949, 6. Oktober), quoted in *Musica,* I (1947), 235.

————. "Über die Lage der Kirchenmusik," *Musik und Kirche,* XX (1950), 123—125.

————. *Die Wiedergeburt der Kirchenmusik.* Kassel, 1953.

Sporn, F. "Ein neuer Komponist in einem alten Kirchenchor," *Musik und Kirche,* VII (1935), 86—88.

Stahl, W. *Musikgeschichte Lübecks.* Vol. II: *Geistliche Musik.* Kassel, 1951—52.

Stein, D. *Die Passionsgeschichte bei Heinrich Schütz und Hugo Distler.* Unpublished manuscript, Kassel, n. d.

Stege, F. "Besuch bei Hugo Distler." Kassel, n. d.

Stever, W. "Singwoche in Ratzeburg," *Musik und Kirche,* VIII (1936), 190.

Strobel, H. and K. W. Bartlett. "Hugo Distler," *Grove's Dictionary of Music and Musicians.* 5th ed., Vol. II, p. 713.

Stuckenschmidt, H. *Neue Musik.* Berlin, 1951.

Sumner, W. *The Organ: Its Evolution, Principles of Construction, and Use.* 2d ed., London, 1955.

Thieme, L. "Abendmusik in St. Katharinen," *Lübeckische Blätter,* 73 (1931), 438.

Typke, Frau H. Unpublished memoir concerning Hugo Distler, dated in Wiesbaden, Nov. 4, 1952.

"Unser Porträt: Hugo Distler," *Kirchenchor,* XVI (1956), 6 f.

Valentin, E. "Vor zehn Jahren starb Hugo Distler," *Zeitschrift für Musik,* CXIII (1952), 630 f.

Wallau, R. *Die Musik in ihrer Gottesbeziehung.* Gütersloh, 1948.

Weiss, E. "Der Dreistimmige Liedsatz," *Musik und Gottesdienst,* VI (1952), 8 f.

"Werke von Distler auf Platten," *Hausmusik,* XXIII (1959), 31.

Woerner, K. *Geschichte der Musik.* Göttingen, 1956.

————. *Musik der Gegenwart.* Mainz, 1949.

————. *Neue Musik in der Entscheidung.* Mainz, 1954.

Music

In addition to the complete works of Hugo Distler, the following scores were consulted.

Bender, Jan. *Now Let All Loudly Sing Praise to God,* cantata for SATB choir, strings, flute, oboe, bassoon, continuo. St. Louis, 1962.

————. *The Sentences for the Seasons.* St. Louis, 1959.

————. *The Word Was Made Flesh,* anthem for SATB choir. St. Louis, 1958.

————. *Twenty Short Organ Pieces.* St. Louis, 1956.

Reda, Siegfried. *Choral- Spiel-Buch für Tasteninstrumente.* Kassel, 1946.

————. *Kleine Orgelstücke.* Kassel, 1948.

————. *Meditationen über Ein Lämmlein geht und trägt die Schuld.* Kassel, 1964.

————. *Vorspiele zu den Psalm-Liedern des EKG.* Kassel, 1957.

Straube, Karl. *Alte Meister des Orgelspiels.* Leipzig, 1926.

Wienhorst, Richard. *A Nativity Cantata.* Chicago, 1956.

————. *Christ Jesus Lay in Death's Strong Bands,* cantata for SATB choir. St. Louis, 1955.

————. *Four Christmas Settings.* St. Louis, 1960.

————. *Mass in four parts.* New York, 1963.

————. *The Seven Words from the Cross.* St. Louis, 1956.